HALLOWEEN

Through Twenty Centuries

BOOKS IN THE

GREAT RELIGIOUS FESTIVALS

SERIES

4000 YEARS OF CHRISTMAS
Earl W. Count

PASSOVER
ITS HISTORY AND TRADITIONS
Theodor H. Gaster

WE GATHER TOGETHER
THE STORY OF THANKSGIVING
Ralph and Adelin Linton

EASTER
ITS STORY AND MEANING
Alan W. Watts

HALLOWEEN
THROUGH TWENTY CENTURIES
Ralph and Adelin Linton

PURIM AND HANUKKAH
IN CUSTOM AND TRADITION
Theodor H. Gaster

RALPH *and* ADELIN LINTON

HENRY SCHUMAN
NEW YORK

Halloween

THROUGH TWENTY CENTURIES

4070

TO CONNIE

BORN ON ALLHALLOWS

PART SAINT

AND

PART WITCH

Contents

Illustrations

. . . For the elemental creatures go
About my table to and fro,
That hurry from unmeasured mind
To rant and rage in flood and wind;
Yet he who treads in measured ways
May surely barter gaze for gaze.
Man ever journeys on with them
After the red-rose-bordered hem.
Ah, faeries, dancing under the moon,
A Druid land, a Druid tune!

—WILLIAM BUTLER YEATS,
"To Ireland in the Coming Times"

HALLOWEEN

Through Twenty Centuries

THE HAG

The hag is astride,
This night for a ride,
Her wild steed and she together;
Through thick and through thin,
Now out, and then in,
Though ne'er so foul be the weather.

A thorn or a burr
She takes for a spur;
With the last of a bramble she rides now.
Through brakes and through briars,
Over ditches and mires
She follows the spirit that guides now.

No beast for his food
Dares now range the wood,
But hush'd in his lair he lies lurking;
While mischief by these,
On land and on seas,
At noon of night are found working.

The storm will arise
And trouble the skies,
This night; and, more for the wonder,
The ghost from the tomb
Affrighted shall come,
Called out by the clap of the thunder.

—ROBERT HERRICK

The Eve of Allhallows

AMONG ALL THE FESTIVALS WHICH WE celebrate today, few have histories stranger than that of Halloween. It is the eve of Allhallows—or Hallowmas or All Saints' Day—and as such it is one of the most solemn festivals of the church. At the same time, it commemorates beings and rites with which the church has always been at war. It is the night when ghosts walk and fairies and goblins are abroad. The witch, with her broomstick and black cat, is seen in every shopwindow. Children double for goblins in practical jokes, and old and young alike try to learn the future by means once forbidden to good Christians. We cannot understand this curious mixture unless we go back into history and unravel the threads from which the present holiday pattern has been woven.

In Latin countries, Halloween is a solemn religious occasion when people attend extra masses and say prayers. The American celebration rests upon Scottish and Irish folk customs which can be traced in direct line from pre-Christian times. Although Halloween has become a night of rollicking fun, superstitious spells, and eerie games which people take only half seriously, its beginnings were quite otherwise. The earliest Halloween celebrations were held by the Druids in honor of Samhain, Lord of the Dead, whose festival fell on November 1. This day was also the Celtic New Year's Day, the beginning of winter and of the time of "the light that loses, the night that wins." The rites performed on this day were eerie enough to thrill the most blasé, but the spirit of fun was sadly lacking.

The Celtic order of Druids originated in Gaul about the second century B.C. By that time the Gauls had had a good deal of contact with the Greeks, and the order may have been modeled on some of the Greek mystery religions. However, its rites also included many savage and primitive elements. The Celtic peoples sprang from the same ancient Indo-European stock as the Greeks and Romans and worshipped many of the same gods and goddesses, although these deities had different names. In addition to honoring Minerva, Apollo, and Mars, the Celts worshipped a Sun God, to whom the horse was sacred, and Samhain, Lord of the Dead. A joint festival was held for the latter two on November 1. The Sun, as ripener of the grain, was thanked for the harvest, now safely stored against the winter, and strengthened for his coming battle with darkness and cold. Samhain, on this night, assembled the souls of all those who had died during the previous year. For their sins these souls had been confined in the bodies of lower animals; on the New Year, their sins being expiated, they were released to go to the Druid heaven.

Horses and human beings were sacrificed at this time. The human victims were usually criminals who had been rounded up for the occasion. These unfortunates were confined in cages of wicker and thatch made in the form of giants or huge animals. The cages were set afire by the priests and the hapless victims roasted alive. This horrid practice was outlawed by Roman command after the conquest of Britain. Suetonius in 61 A.D. ordered the groves of human sacrifice and augury destroyed.

In spite of this suppression, the old rites survived for centuries in attenuated form. A weird survival of the Druid burnings is reported from medieval Europe, where black cats were put into wicker cages and burned alive on Halloween. The cat sacrifices were made in the conviction that the cats were the familiars of witches or even the witches themselves, since it was commonly believed that witches often transformed themselves into cats.

In Britain, horses were sacrificed at the feast of Samhain as late as 400 A.D. Even after the Christians had taken over the pagan temples and consecrated them to the worship of the Christian God, oxen continued to be sacrificed on Hallowmas, sometimes being led down the church aisle to the altar. Bede's *Ecclesiastical History of the English People* quotes a letter from Pope Gregory the Great in the sixth century to Abbot Mellitus, instructing him to tell Augustine, the first Archbishop of Canterbury, that "the temples of the idols in that nation ought not to be destroyed but that the idols should. That the sacrifice of oxen in pagan worship should be allowed to continue, but that this should be done in honor of the saints and sacred relics."

The final incorporation of the feast of Samhain into the Christian calendar took somewhat longer. Allhallows is a feast of the church celebrated in honor of all the saints, known or unknown. The earliest report of a general commemoration of martyrs mentions one in Antioch on the Sunday after Pentecost. In 609, Pope Boniface IV consecrated the old Roman temple called the Pantheon and dedicated it to the Blessed Virgin and all the martyrs. The feast of St. Mary and the Martyrs was held on May 13, 610. In the eighth century, Pope Gregory III dedicated an oratory in St. Peter's to all the saints and fixed the anniversary as November 1. In 834, Pope Gregory IV established this festival in the calendar to be observed by all churches.

All Saints' Day was introduced into the church calendar because the year was not long enough to make it possible to dedicate a special day for each saint of the Catholic Church. Also, it was recognized that many martyrs and other faithful who were worthy of sainthood had died unrecognized, so that this day honors the unknown saints as well as those who have been canonized. That the day chosen was one already associated in the popular mind with a thronging of spirits of the dead was quite in line with the church policy of incorporating harmless pagan folk ideas.

The Eve of Allhallows

Outside the church, the belief in Halloween as a gathering time for unsanctified as well as sanctified spirits seems to have continued with little change. To the ghosts originally assembled by the Lord of the Dead were added troops of goblins and fairies. This was logical enough, for the fairy folk had their beginnings in an exceedingly ancient, even pre-Celtic, cult of the dead. The fairy host as it first appears in Scottish and Irish legend was not made up of gauzy-winged midgets but of beings larger and more beautiful than men. They were the ghosts of ancient kings and heroes mingled with elder gods. The burial mounds of the Neolithic and Bronze Age folk were their dwellings, and they rode forth on the feast of Samhain to take a scornful look at the feeble folk who kept the land they once ruled. Stunned by the sound of Christian bells and shriveled by holy water, the fairy folk dwindled to "little people," whose only vestige of their ancient state was that they still kept their ancient dwelling places. Even so dazzling a figure of romance as Maeve, the warrior queen of Connacht, survived only as the fragile Queen Mab of the English poets.

Even more characteristic than the inclusion of goblins and fairies in the Halloween picture was the association of the festival with witchcraft. Long after the church had triumphed over organized paganism, country people everywhere in Europe continued their ancient practice of placating local spirits and strengthening fertility by magical rites. Their magic was as much "white" as "black." The parish priests tolerated these doings even if they did

7

not approve of them, and the villagers themselves saw no conflict with Christianity. In the later Middle Ages, the church began to take a stronger stand against such pagan survivals, and with the 'Reformation they were classed as heresy.

The result was the emergence of witchcraft as a more or less organized cult in opposition to the church. Much of its ritual was a travesty of Christian rites, but it also incorporated many of the ancient beliefs and practices, among them the ancient sacred days. Halloween became the great witch night. The Prince of Darkness and his cohorts, the witches and warlocks, gathered to mock the church's festival of All Saints by unholy revels of their own. In Germany, their meeting place for the Great Sabbath was the mountain called the Brocken; in Sweden, the Blocksberg; in France, the Forest of Ardennes. In Great Britain it seems that any old church, ruined abbey, or megalithic monument on a lonely heath would serve.

On the eve of Samhain, the pagan Celts lit bonfires on the hills to welcome the winter season and ward off evil spirits. In dwellings all the cooking fires were extinguished and new ones kindled in token of the new year. The idea that ghosts and spirits fear fire is widespread, and with the rise of the witch cult fire became the favorite weapon against the powers of darkness. The burning of witches was a rite of purification even more than of punishment.

The peasants of Scotland and Ireland still build fires on the hillsides on Halloween. They also plait their pitchforks with straw, set them on fire, and wave them aloft to singe the brooms of any witches who may happen to be hovering near by. The Scandinavian peasants have a similar custom, believing that blazing, straw-laden pitchforks and thrown disks of burning straw will drive the witches back to the Blocksberg, the mountain where the queen of the witches dwells.

In Austria, the witch night is May Eve, or Walpurgis Night, April 30. The town of Benevento in Italy was supposed to be the scene of one of the Great Sabbaths held every seven years by Satan and his cohorts. The peasants of the region still remember this, and on Midsummer Eve, (St. John's Eve in the church calendar) they purge the land of witches. The inhabitants of Sannio, near Benevento, store and dry timber for this occasion all winter. The logs are pared and shaped into torches, which are consecrated by the priest. After nightfall on the twenty-third of June, the peasants wind their way to the church on the hilltop, bearing blazing torches and singing ancient melodies. The witches, who return to their meeting place, are singed in the consecrated fire and fly away, leaving the village purged of evil for another year.

In spite of its pagan accompaniments, Allhallows was retained at the time of the Reformation in the calendars of the Church of England and of many Lutheran groups. Halloween has a special significance for Protestants, since it was on that day, in 1517, that Martin Luther posted his epochmaking ninety-five theses on the door of the castle church at Wittenberg. These theses were an attack upon the practice of purchasing indulgences. The church's penitential system required that, in addition to their repentance and confession, sinners must perform acts of penance. If these were not performed, the sin had to be expiated in purgatory. The indulgences exempted those who could afford them from penance in this world and the next.

The sale of indulgences was begun as a means of raising money needed for building churches, including St. Peter's at Rome. However, the system was abused by greedy prelates. The Archbishop of Mainz was doing a brisk and profitable business in pardons—a fact which aroused Luther's indignation. "Concerning indulgences," said Luther, "although they are the very merits of Christ and his saints, and are therefore by all means to be received with reverence, they are nevertheless made the most shameful agents of avarice."

Luther wrote out his ninety-five theses against this abuse by hand. It was customary to post notices on church doors, which served as community bulletin boards. He chose Halloween night because he knew that the townsfolk, the university students, and many pilgrims would be coming to the church that night. The castle church was called the Church of All Saints, because the pious Elector, Frederick the Wise, had collected in it over 5,000 saintly relics: a lock of St. Elizabeth's hair, part of St. Euphemia's head, a tooth of St. Beatrice, and so forth. The faithful made pilgrimages to do homage to these sacred objects, particularly on the eve of All Saints.

Although he knew that his theses would be seen

by many people on this particular night, Luther was not prepared for the enthusiastic reception which they received. Apparently resentment had long been smoldering against a doctrine which favored the rich so heavily. The practice of selling indulgences was abolished soon after. By that time, however, other differences had arisen or flared and the Reformation was under way.

Soul! Soul! for a soul cake!
I pray, good mistress, for a soul cake!
An apple or a pear, or a plum or a cherry
Any good thing to make us merry.
One for Peter, two for Paul,
Three for him who made us all.
Up with the kettle and down with the pan.
Give us good alms and we'll be gone.

All Souls' Day

ALL SOULS' DAY FOLLOWS ALL SAINTS' Day, on November 2. This festival of the Catholic Church is set apart for those who, although they have not suffered martyrdom or achieved sainthood, have died in the faith. It is dedicated particularly to those who have passed away during the preceding year and whose souls can be helped on their journey through purgatory by the prayers of the faithful.

This feast of general intercession for the souls of the dead was originated by Odilo, Abbot of Cluny, France, who died in 1048. Odilo ordered this observance in his own Cluniac monasteries, which numbered over three hundred, and the custom spread from there to other congregations. By the end of the thirteenth century, the celebration of All Souls' Day was practically universal. This festival was abolished in the Church of England at the time of the Reformation but is now observed by Anglo-Catholics as well as Roman Catholics.

There is a widespread belief that the spirits of the dead return to visit their former homes on one particular day of the year. Most of the pre-Christian cults celebrated a Day of the Dead, and it is natural that the Christian church should also set apart a special day for the souls of its faithful. Many of the pagan attitudes toward this day have been retained in some of the more primitive Catholic communities; for example, the preparing of food and offerings for the returned ghosts.

In ancient Egypt, the Day of the Dead was celebrated at the time of the winter solstice. This feast was in honor of Osiris, the god whose death symbolized the death of vegetation. The golden cow, representative of Isis, the sorrowing wife, was carried seven times around the temple while the people wailed and beat their breasts to symbolize their sorrow for the death of the god.

On this anniversary of the death of Osiris the souls of the dead returned to the land of the living. Food was spread in the houses for the homecoming spirits, and at dusk rows of oil lamps were fastened outside all the housefronts. They were kept burning throughout the night, making the streets as bright as day, so that the wandering ghosts would have no difficulty in finding their way home.

In Greece, the festival of the dead was held in February and was the third day of the Dionysiac feast of the *Anthesteria*. The first day was that of the "cask-opening," when the casks of new wine were brought up and opened. The next day was that of the "pitcher feast," involving elaborate banquets and drinking contests, at the end of which each guest poured out the remaining wine in his pitcher as a libation to the god Dionysus. After these two days of merriment and revelry, the festival closed with the day of the "feast of pots," dedicated to dead souls. (This contrast in mood may be compared with that which characterizes our Shrove Tuesday and Ash Wednesday.) The festival took its name from the custom of setting out pots of cooked vegetables and grains to sustain the spirits who swarmed up into the land of the living on this day. The Greeks feared to offend their ghostly visitors, but they regarded the invasion without enthusiasm. They smeared their doorposts with pitch in an attempt to keep the spirits away and chewed hawthorn leaves as a protection against ghostly contact. The temples of the gods were tightly closed during this period lest the ghosts find their way in and linger there beyond their allotted time. At the end of the feast the people chased the spirits of the departed from their houses with a formula of exorcism: "Begone ye Keres, Anthesteria is over."

The Romans celebrated a feast for the dead called the *dies parentales*, or *Parentalia*. This also was held in February, continuing from the thirteenth to the twenty-first, during which time all temples were closed and marriages were forbidden.

The *Parentalia* was chiefly a private festival, in which families brought offerings of milk, wine, and honey to the tombs of their dead and decorated them with garlands of flowers. Roses and violets were the blooms particularly favored by the spirits of the dead. On the last day, the twenty-first, the public festival for the dead, called the *Feralia*, was held.

A very ancient ritual of the dead, probably borrowed from the Etruscans, was celebrated in early Rome from May 9 to 13. It was called the *Lemuria*, which was also the word for ghosts.

In medieval times criers dressed entirely in black marched through the streets on All Souls' Day ringing a mournful bell and calling upon all good people to remember the poor souls in purgatory and to say prayers for them. In London, the church bells used to toll all day long on November 2, until Queen Elizabeth ordered this clangorous custom stopped. She felt that it was popish and also found it offensive to royal ears.

Throughout England the "soulers" used to walk the streets on this day, singing and begging. Alms were given them, in return for which it was understood that the soulers were to say extra prayers for the dead relatives of the donors. The more prayers said, the more rapid the passage of the dead soul through purgatory.

The bakers' shops were filled with soulcakes—square buns decorated with currants, which were the special delicacy for this day, just as hot cross buns are for Good Friday. The soulers chanted, "A soul cake, a soul cake, have mercy on all Christian souls for a soul cake!" or the more elaborate version given at the opening of this chapter.

In Yorkshire the bakers made special *sæumas* (soul mass) loaves, which they gave to all their customers. One loaf was kept in each house during the year for good luck and as a charm against death.

In Shropshire it was the lads who went around "souling," making quite a lark of it. The following is one of the old Shropshire souling songs:

Here's two or three hearty lads, standing hard by,
We are come a-souling, good nature to try,
We are come a-souling, as well doth appear,
And all that we soul for is ale and strong beer.

Go down to your cellar, and there you shall find
Both ale, beer, and brandy and, best of all, wine;
And when we have got it, O then you shall see,
And when we have drunk it, how merry we'll be.

I pray, my good mistress, don't tarry to spin,
Look for a jug to draw some drink in,
And when you are drawing, don't let your heart fail,
But draw us a jug of your bonny brown ale.

In seventeenth-century Ireland, the peasants would go to the houses of the wealthy on this day, asking for alms with which to buy luxuries for the feast in honor of St. Columba or Columkille. St. Columba was an Irishman of royal lineage who became a Christian in the sixth century and converted the Picts. He founded a monastery on Iona Island.

Halloween

In France, November 2 is called the *Jour des Morts*, Day of the Dead. People stream to the cemeteries to decorate the graves of their loved ones. The shops sell wreaths and garlands of immortelles, or everlastings, some in their natural color and others dyed pink, blue, or purple. The cemeteries become vivid masses of color.

In southern Italy in the fourteenth century, every family prepared a special feast for its dead members on All Souls' Day. In Salerno especially this custom reached elaborate heights. There a table was set and laid with a bountiful meal. Then all the members of the household went to the church and stayed there the entire day, leaving the house open for the ghosts. It was a very bad omen if any of the food remained uneaten when the family returned, for this meant that the ghosts were expressing disapproval. If they refused to partake of the family's hospitality, they might work evil against its relatives. As a matter of fact, there was seldom any food left when the family returned; the practice was known to all the surrounding villages and on the morning of All Souls' Day thieves and beggars from near and far gathered on the outskirts of the town. When all the good people were in church, they swarmed into the town and enjoyed a fine feast. The church banned this custom in the fifteenth century, proclaiming that it smacked of paganism. No doubt the housewives of Salerno were relieved at no longer having to cook dinners for all the thieves in the countryside.

All Souls' Day

In Latin America, notably in Mexico, All Souls' Day, or *El Día de los Muertos*, is an important national holiday. All Saints' Day, *El Día de Todos Santos*, is not the solemn occasion it is in most Catholic countries but is merely a prelude to the great Day of the Dead. November 1 is the time when the *difuntos chiquitos*, the dead children, return to visit their homes. On Halloween night, special *ofrendas*, or offerings, of cakes and confections are set out for the *angelitos*, the child angels, and also a toy or two. To make sure that the children will find their way home, some parents shoot off firecrackers in front of their houses. In certain villages of Santa Cruz and Puebla, petals of the *zempasuchitl*, a yellow marigold which is the special flower of the dead, are scattered by the family from the cemetery to the door of the house. The ghosts can find their way by following this yellow path. Halloween as it is celebrated in the United States is unknown south of the border, but the belief is prevalent that it is a night when ghosts and spirits are abroad. The men and boys go from house to house and sing *alabanzas*, or hymns to the dead, before the *ofrendas* laid out by each household. For fear of the ghosts, they are careful to stay in groups and to avoid lonely roads.

The Day of the Dead, November 2, however, is the important holiday. It is not so solemn an occasion as its name would indicate, but for the most part is a joyous *fiesta* to which the children especially look forward eagerly. The Mexicans are fatalists who accept death uncomplainingly and can joke about it even when they are grieving for their loved ones. Skulls and skeletons are the motifs of this holiday. Made of sugar or pastry, they leer from all the bakeshop windows. Street venders hawk macabre toys for the children, skeletons with clay skull heads and jointed legs which dance grotesquely, little jack-in-the-box coffins from which a skeleton jumps when a string is pulled. Girls buy necktie pins in the shape of skeletons with gleaming eyes and dangling ribs as presents for their sweethearts. The *panes de muertos*, or bread of the dead, is another special feature of this day. These are flat breads made in the shape of men and women or of animals and dressed in garments of colored icings.

In Europe, in the fifteenth century, the church banned the custom of offering food to the dead on All Souls' Day as a heathen practice, but the good Catholics of Mexico continue to make their *ofrendas* for their departed members. Although this food is prepared for the dead, when the ghosts have appreciated the honor and partaken of the feast in spirit, the family happily eats what is left.

The most exotic and beautiful of the ceremonies of the Day of the Dead is held in the Tarascan island village of Janitzio on Lake Patzcuaro. The ceremony begins on the evening of November 1. The women and children go to bed at sunset, for they must rise at midnight. The men go about singing *alabanzas*. At midnight the women rise and dress themselves and their children in *fiesta* garments. They pack baskets of food for the *ofrendas*. The special delicacy prepared for the ghosts here is roasted wild duck. Several days before this event the men go out in their canoes and hunt the ducks, which feed in great numbers on Lake Patzcuaro. They kill the ducks by circling them with their boats and, when the birds take to the air, harpooning them with spears, a feat of skill which northern duck hunters could probably never match.

At midnight on November 1, laden with food and the materials for decorating the graves, women and children climb the steep paths to the hillside cemetery. Over each grave is placed an arch garlanded with *zempasuchitl* and hung with *panes de muertos*. Candles are lighted on each grave, their combined glow so bright that the flickering gleam lights up the lake and can be seen from the mainland. The tourists who flock to the island to see this ceremony take pictures by the candlelight.

The women and children sit all night in the golden candlelight beside their gaily decked graves, giving warmth and companionship to the inhabitants. The men and grown boys linger on the outskirts of the cemetery, leaning against the wall singing *alabanzas* and taking frequent nips from the bottles of *pulque* which are passed from hand to hand. When dawn comes up over Lake Patzcuaro, the women open their baskets, offer the food to heaven, to the souls of the dead, and then to each other. Well fed and happy, they leave the cemetery in the morning light.

Yes! let the rich deride, the proud disdain,
The simple pleasures of the lowly train;
To me more dear, congenial to my heart,
One native charm, than all the gloss of art.

—OLIVER GOLDSMITH, "The Deserted Village"

"To Burn Their Nits and Pou Their Stocks"

IN BOTH PAGAN AND CHRISTIAN TIMES,
the period from nightfall on the thirty-first of October to sunset on the second of November seems
to have held special significance. It is a time when
the unseen world of the spirits is closer to this mun-
dane sphere than at any other point in the calendar. On this night the souls of the dead return. The
mischievous elves and trolls and the evil witches
are also about. Since these spirits can see into the
future, all sorts of divination games are included in
the order of Halloween festivities. In Scotland and
Ireland particularly these games were popular
among the peasantry, and it is largely from these
countries that the Halloween customs of the
United States have been taken. Although these
games were undertaken for sport, there is enough
of the old superstition left to give a spine-tingling

feeling that perhaps the spirits are directing the omens of the nuts and apples and other charms and that their prophecies may come true.

The imprint of the ancient Druidical festival is still felt in this holiday. In some parts of Ireland it is still called *Oidhche Shamhna*, the Vigil of Samhain. The fires which the Scots light in their hills are called Samhnagan. These names are merely survivals, the significance of which has been long forgotten. The Hallowmas fires are not for Samhain, Druid god, but for Halloween gaiety and a defiant welcome to the winter season, although some of the old folks may recall that the flames are useful in driving away witches.

In the Highlands on the last day of autumn the children sally forth to gather dry ferns and branches for the fires. Logs and firewood are too precious in this country to be burned for frivolity, but the various households vie with one another to have the biggest blaze on Halloween night. The gleanings are piled on the highest spot near the house. Whole districts gleam with fires in the evening, the glow reflected in the lochs and lighting up the hills.

In Wales, where Halloween is a more solemn evening than in the north countries and is more preoccupied with thoughts of death, the Halloween fires have a somewhat sinister significance. When the fire is dying down to embers, each member of the family throws into the rosy circle a white stone marked with his or her name. Then they march around the fire saying their prayers, after which they go to bed and probably do not sleep too well.

In the morning, they go out to reclaim their stones. If anyone's stone is missing from the ashes, it means that he will die before the next Halloween.

In Scotland and Ireland, however, the mood is not so solemn and the charms and omens are mostly built about love predictions. The country folk spend the evening gathered together at some hospitable cottage for games and feasts. Nuts and apples are the main refreshments. There is usually plenty of ale and whiskey, "a social glass of strunt," as Robert Burns calls it.

The genial and eerie goings-on in Scotland on Halloween have been immortalized in charming ribald verse by Burns. His "Tam O'Shanter" and "Halloween" are the two great poems of this holiday.

The first tells of the adventures of Tam, who tarried too long at the tavern in Ayr after market day. He did not start home to his good wife, Kate, until the wizard hour between night and morning. As Tam, mounted on his good mare, Meg, passed the Alloway Kirk, he was amazed to see its windows blazing with light. He stopped to peer within and there beheld an "unco sight." Witches and warlocks were cavorting in a wild dance, with auld Nick himself playing the bagpipe for the revels.

> He screwed the pipes, and gart them skirl *
> Till roof and rafter a' did dirl.†
> Coffins stood round, like open presses,
> That shawed the dead in their last dresses.

* Made them scream. † Vibrate.

The altar was heaped with a grisly variety of witches' charms. Some of the witches were old crones, but there was one winsome wench whom Tam recognized as a village girl called Nannie. She was a novice, newly joined to this unholy group, but she later, Burns tells us, became a powerful witch who withered crops, killed cattle and caused shipwrecks. Nannie was dressed in a fine smock of Paisley which, unfortunately, she had outgrown. But it was her best and she was proud of it and wore it for this occasion, even though it was too short to answer the purpose of such a garment. This is the famous *cutty sark* or short shirt. A famous ship and later a famous whiskey have since been named after Nannie's outgrown smock.

> Her cutty sark, o' Paisley harn,
> That while a lassie she had worn
> In longitude though sorely scanty,
> It was her best, and she was vauntie.
> Ah! little kenn'd thy reverend grannie,
> That sark she coft for her wee Nannie,
> Wi twa pund Scots ('twas a' her riches),
> Wad ever graced a dance of witches!

Tam was so fascinated by Nannie's dance that he lost his reason altogether and roared out, "Weel done, Cutty-sark!" and in an instant all was dark. All the evil spirits took out after poor Tam and his mare, "wi mony an eldritch skreech and hollow." Had it not been for the well-known fact that no witch can cross a running stream, Tam would have fared ill that night. The witches caught up with

him when his mare was halfway across the bridge
over the River Doon.

> Ae spring brought off her master hale,
> But left behind her ain gray tale.
> The carlin claught her by the rump,
> And left poor Maggie scarce a stump.

Burns's "Halloween" is a treasury of Scottish
folklore, describing in lively and somewhat coarse
verse the games and superstitions of Halloween in
the highlands. Most of the games are a kind of divination sport, to determine the names of the players'
future mates. The elves and fairies and witches,
who know the future, are abroad that night. It is
elfin fingers that direct the prophecies to be read in
nuts and apples. Wandering ghosts produce appari-
tions and make dire prophecies of death.

> Upon that night, when fairies light
>   On Cassilis Downans dance
> Or owre the lays, in splendid blaze
>   On sprightly coursers prance;
> Or for Colean the route is ta'en,
>   Beneath the moon's pale beams;
> There up the cove, to stray and rove,
>   Among the rocks and streams
>   To sport that night.

> Among the bonny winding banks,
>   Where Doon runs, wimplin' clear,
> Where Bruce ance ruled the martial ranks,
>   And shook his Carrick spear,

Halloween

Some merry, friendly country-folks,
　　Together did convene,
To burn their nits and pou their stocks,
　　And haud their Halloween
　　　　　　Fu' blithe that night.

"To burn their nits" refers to the custom of naming nuts for a boy and girl who are lovers and placing the christened nuts side by side on the hearth. The reaction of the nuts to the heat of the fire foretells the progress of the love affair. If one catches fire and the other does not, the one whose nut flames will love madly and be rejected. If one or both nuts crack and jump into the fire, the lovers will quarrel and separate. If both nuts burn quietly together, the pair will be happily married within the year.

Here is Burns's description of this ceremony:

The auld guidwife's weel hoordit nits,
　　Are round and round divided,
And monie lads' and lassies' fates
　　Are there that night decided:
Some kindle coothie, side by side,
　　And burn the gither trimly;
Some start awa', wi' saucy pride,
　　And jump out-owre the chimlie
　　　　　　Fu' high that night.

Jean slips in twa wi' tentie ee;
　　Wha 'twas she wadna tell;
But this is Jock, and this is me,
　　She says in to hersel:

"To Burn Their Nits and Pou Their Stocks"

> He bleezed owre her, and she owre him,
>   As they wad never mair part;
> Till, fuff! he started up the lum,*
>   And Jean had e'en a sair heart
>   To see 't that night.

"Pou their stocks" refers to another popular divination game—pulling the kale. The lads and lasses go out hand in hand to a kale or cabbage patch. The charm is stronger if they go to the patch of a stranger who has not given them permission to pull his kale. They shut their eyes and in the dark grasp at random for a stalk and pull. If the stalk is tall and straight, the future mate will be strong and well built. If it is shriveled or crooked, the kale puller will marry a hunchback or a sickly person. If a good deal of earth clings to the roots, the marriage will be a wealthy one. If the roots come out bare and clean, the future spouse will be able to give nothing but love. Then the young people cut open their stalks and taste the *custoc*, or pith. If it is sweet and tender, the mate will be kind and gentle; if it is sour or bitter, the spouse is likely to have a disagreeable disposition.

> "Then, straught or crooked, yirt or nane,
>   They roar and cry a' throu'ther;
> The very wee things, todlin' rin,
>   Wi' stocks ou-owre their shouther;
> And gif the custoc's sweet or sour,
>   Wi joctelegs † they taste them;
> Syne cosily, aboon the door,
>   Wi canny care, they've placed them
>   To lie that night."

* Chimney.   † Knives.

Halloween

John Gregorson Campbell,* minister of Tiree, re-counted a tale told him personally of an incident at the Halloween kale pulling. A girl who lived in Skye was in love with a sailor lad who had shipped off to the East Indies. Although her heart was al-ready pledged, she went with the other young people to the kale patch on Halloween night to pull her stalk. As she grasped the plant, she felt something hurtle through the dark and hit it. She pulled the kale, which proved to be straight and tall with rich dirt clinging to the root, but embed-ded in the stalk was a knife. All the other young people denied having thrown it or knowing to whom it belonged.

When her lover returned some months later, he told her that on Halloween night he was leaning over the side of the ship, thinking of her and of the festivities which were going on in Skye and feeling lovelorn and homesick. He had his knife in his hand, for he had been mending some rope. In his reverie he let the knife slip through his fingers and it fell with a splash into the sea. The girl produced the knife she had found in the kale stalk. Her lover recognized it as the very one he had lost in the tropical ocean.

Another Halloween game which Burns tells of is one in which the girls go into a field in the dark and with their eyes closed pull a stalk of oats. If the head of the grain—"the tap-pickle mast"—is gone, it means that the girl will not be a virgin when she

* John Gregorson Campbell, *Witchcraft and Second Sight in the Scottish Highlands*. MacLeod; Glasgow, 1902.

goes to the marriage bed. Here is Burns's description:

> The lasses staw frae 'mang them a'
>   To pou their stalks o' corn;
> But Rab slips out and jinks about,
>   Behint the muckle thorn:
> He grippet Nelly hard and fast;
>   Loud skirl'd a' the lasses;
> But her tap-pickle mast was lost,
>   When kitlin' in the fause-house *
>   Wi' him that night.

There are many ways in which a girl may learn the name of her future husband or see his apparition. One method is for the unmarried girl to go off alone to a *kiln*, an outhouse or barn, taking with her a *clue*, or ball of yarn. She throws the ball over a rafter or crossbeam, keeping an end of the yarn in her hand. Then she begins to wind it. When the yarn catches or jerks, the girl asks, "Who is down there at the end of my little rope?" The apparition of her future husband, who is tugging at the *clue*, replies, giving his name.

Campbell tells of an incident at a Halloween gathering when the village tailor, knowing that some of the girls would be trying this stunt, hid in the kiln. When a ball of yarn came flying over the crossbeam in the dark, he gave it a gentle tug. "Who is there at the end of my little rope?" quavered the girl. "The devil!" answered the tailor in a sepulchral voice. The girl fled with a shriek and was so terrified that she would not walk with

* Cuddling in the haystack.

any of the lads during the following year for fear that he would prove to be the devil as prophesied.

Burns describes this practice also:

> But Merran sat behint their backs,
>   Her thoughts on Andrew Bell;
> She lea'es them gashin' at their cracks,
>   And slips out by hersel':
> She through the yard the nearest taks,
>   And to the kiln goes then,
> And darklins graipit for the bauks,*
>   And in the blue-clue throws them,
>   Right fear't that night.
>
> And aye she win't and aye she swat,
>   I wat she made nae jaukin',
> Till something held within the pat,
>   Guid Lord! but she was quakin'!
> But whether 'twas the deil himsel,
>   Or whether 'twas a bauk-en',
> Or whether it was Andrew Bell,
>   She didna wait on talkin'
>   To spier † that night.

Another divination practice calls for a girl to go alone into a dark room carrying a lighted candle, an apple, a knife, and a mirror. She cuts the apple into nine pieces; then, gazing into the mirror, she eats eight pieces, spears the ninth one on the point of the knife and holds it over her shoulder. The apparition of her future husband comes to take the apple section and his face is mirrored in the glass beside her own. In some versions the girl is supposed to comb her hair during this process.

* Crossbeams.   † Inquire.

"To Burn Their Nits and Pou Their Stocks"

In Burns's poem, little Jenny proposes to try this method:

> Wee Jenny to her grannie says,
>   "Wi ye go wi' me, grannie?
> I'll eat the apple at the glass
>   I got from Uncle Johnnie."

But grannie is so indignant at the child's indulging in such sport that she puffs her pipe too hard and burns her best apron with a cinder. She tells Jenny:

> "Nae doubt but ye may get a sight!
>   Great cause ye hae to fear it :
> For mony a ane has gotten a fright,
>   And lived and died deleeret
>   On sic a night."

And grannie goes on to tell horrid tales of things that have happened on Halloween. Jamie Fleck, however, claims that he is not afraid, "for it was a' but nonsense." He proves this by going out in the fields to try his fortune with hempseed. This is done by scattering hempseed in the Halloween dark and saying the magical verse:

> Hemp-seed, I saw thee,
> And her that is to be my lass
> Come after me and draw thee.

A vision of the man's future wife then comes up behind him to reap the magically grown hemp. Jamie

Halloween

. . . whistled up Lord Lennox march
　To keep his courage cheery;
Although his hair began to arch,
　He was sae fley'd and eerie;
Till presently he hears a squeak,
　And then a grane and gruntle;
He by his shouther gae a keek,
　And tumbled wi' a wintle
　　　　　Out-owre that night.

He roar'd a horrid murder-shout,
　In dreadfu' desperation!
And young and auld cam runnin' out
　To hear the sad narration;
He swore 'twas hilchin Jean M'Craw,
　Or crouchie Merran Humphie,
Till, stop! she trotted through them a'
　And wha was it but grumphie *
　　　　　Asteer that night.

In another method of divination for the lovelorn, the girl goes late and alone to a stream, or *burn*, and dips her left sleeve into the cold running water. When she returns home, she takes off her *sark* and hangs it up for the sleeve to dry. During the night an apparition of her intended will come to turn the sleeve. If she can stay awake to watch, she will see him. If she fails to see him, it is because she has dozed off at the time that he appeared.

Burns describes how Leezie, a widow eager for another husband, tries this charm.

* The pig.

34

1. Halloween at the time of Robert Burns.

"Some merry friendly country folk
Together did convene
To burn their nits, an' pou their stocks
And hand their Halloween."

(Courtesy of the Bettmann Archive, New York)

2. *The witches' Sabbath, by Hans Baldung.*

(Courtesy of The Metropolitan Museum of Art, New York)

"To Burn Their Nits and Pou Their Stocks"

A wanton widow Leezie was,
  As canty as a kittlin;
But och! that night amang the shaws,
  She got a fearfu' settlin'!
She through the whins, and by the cairn,
  And owre the hill gaed scrievin,
Whare three lairds' lands met at a burn
  To dip her left sark-sleeve in,
            Was bent that night.

Amang the brackens, on the brae,
  Between her and the moon,
The deil, or else an outler quey,*
  Gat up and gae a croon:
Poor Leezie's heart maist lap the hool! †
  Near lav' rock height she jumpit;
But mist a fit, and in the pool
  Out-owre the lugs she plumpit,
            Wi' a plunge that night.

There is also the game of the three luggies. Three dishes are ranged on the hearth: one full of clean water, one of dirty water, and one empty. The person who wishes to know his future is blindfolded. He then gropes for the dishes. If he dips a finger in the clean water, he will marry a virgin; if in the dirty water, he will marry a widow; if an empty dish, he will not marry at all. This test was usually tried three times to verify the prophecy, the dishes being shifted around after each try.

Burns tells of Uncle John's sad experience with the *toom* (empty) dish, which meant that no woman would say "yes" to him that year:

* Spirit.   † Burst its case.

Halloween

In order, on the clean harth-stane,
    The luggies three are ranged,
And every time great care is ta'en
    To see them duly changed:
Auld Uncle John, wha wedlock joys
    Sin' Mar's year did desire,
Because he gat the toom dish thrice,
    He heaved them on the fire
                In wrath that night.

All these games were undertaken in fun, but there was enough belief in the reality of the ghosts and spirits which ordered the spells to give zest to the party. Until,

Wi' merry sangs, and friendly cracks,
    I wat they didna weary:
And unco tales, and funny jokes,
    Their sports were cheap and cheery;
Till butter'd so'ns, wi fragrant lunt,*
    Set a' their gabs a-steerin';
Syne, wi a social glass o' strunt,†
    They parted aff careerin'
                Fu' blythe that night.

* Smoke.   † Spirits.

Farewell, rewards and fairies,
　　Good housewives now may say,
For now foul sluts in dairies
　　Do fare as well as *they*.
And though they sweep their hearths no less
　　Than maids were wont to do,
Yet who of late for cleanliness,
　　Finds sixpence in her shoe?

—BISHOP OF OXFORD AND NORWICH (seventeenth
century), "Farewell to the Fairies"

Halloween in Ireland

IN SCOTLAND AND IRELAND, THE LAST
strongholds of the Druids, Halloween has had the
sportive superstitious attributes which Americans
have come to associate with this holiday. In Ireland,
it is the time when ghosts walk, when the fruitful
year dies and winter begins, but it also is a night
when the fairies are about. The Irish imagination
dwells more on the fantastic and capricious than
on the darker powers. In Eire it is fairies, the *Sidhe*
(pronounced "shee"), rather than witches and
devils, which dominate the folklore. The fairies, although invisible, are always about. One should
never throw slops out of a door or window without calling to the fairies to take care, for they
might be passing by and resent the soiling of their
gay caps and clothes.

Anthropologists trace the origin of the fairies to
an ancient cult of the dead. To the Neolithic and

Bronze Age peoples of the British Isles, the ancestral spirits were powerful and ever present. It was to honor these spirits that they raised giant stones and built mounds over tombs. When Christianity replaced the old religion, both the ancestral spirits and the old gods shrank to "little people," and new myths were made to explain them. One of these is that God made fairies on the third day of Creation, out of earth, air, and water, but He did not give them souls. Another is that at the time of Lucifer's rebellion some angels sided with Lucifer and were cast into hell, where they became demons; others remained true to God, the Father, and stayed in heaven, sharing the celestial glory; the indifferent ones, who failed to take sides in the quarrel, were cast out and condemned to dwell on earth as fairies until Judgment Day.

Fairies are immortal; that is, they do not die as humans do, but on Judgment Day they will be annihilated, whereas good mortals will have eternal life. For this reason, fairies, though not malevolent as witches are, are jealous of mortals and like to play tricks on them. Fairies are often generous and helpful toward mortals, however. There are many fairy stories based on the theme of the mortal man who falls in love with a mermaid or a wood sprite, marries her, and tries to help her to win a human soul.

It is said that Finvarra, the great chief of the fairies, sought out St. Columkille, the first Celtic missionary, to beg him to intercede for the fairies and give them hope of salvation. The saint assured the fairy chief that this was impossible; the fairy people were doomed to extinction.

The fairies, like the witches, held their meetings on May Eve, Midsummer Eve, and November Eve (Halloween), but their meetings were gay festivals with dancing and merriment. Midsummer Eve, the Eve of St. John, was the date of their greatest revel. Families with pretty daughters kept them locked up on this night, for the fairy men were out looking for mortal maidens whom they could carry off as brides.

3.   *The rescue from the fairies. From Mrs. Hall's* Irish Sketches.

Fairies often stole newborn babies out of their cradles and left a fairy changeling child behind. They also bewitched adults, as in the stories of *The Frog Prince* and *The Sleeping Beauty*. The best time to rescue the victims of such enchantment was on Halloween. The rescuer had to obtain from some fairy doctor or wise woman a special ointment which, when rubbed on the eyelids, enabled the user to see the fairies, who were ordinarily invisible. He then stood at a crossroads on Halloween and waited for the fairy troop to pass on the way to their November Eve dance. Their approach was always heralded by a gust of wind. As the fairies passed, the watcher threw on them a handful of dust from the road or a splash of milk from a jug which he brought with him. The fairies were then obliged to surrender any human being whom they had bewitched or stolen.

Most of the divination and fortune-telling games which Burns described as being played at Halloween gatherings in the cottages in the Scottish highlands were also played by the Irish countryfolk around their peat fires.

The Irish have a somewhat more macabre version of the game of the three luggies. They range three saucers on the hearth: one filled with clean water, one filled with earth, and one filled with meal. If the blindfolded player puts his hand in the clean water, it means that he will live to see another Halloween; if he touches the earth, he is going to die before the year is out; if he touches the meal, he will have a long and prosperous life.

Another Halloween divination game from Ireland is that of "throwing the shoe." The player takes off one of his shoes and tosses it over the cottage roof. In whatever direction the shoe points, the wearer will go. If it points toward the house, he will stay at home. If it points away from the house, the wearer will travel in that direction. If it lands sole uppermost, it portends misfortune or even death.

The jack-o'-lanterns which children carve from pumpkins for Halloween are also an Irish tradition. To be sure, there were no pumpkins in the old country, but outsized rutabagas, potatoes, or turnips were hollowed out, carved with grotesque faces, and lighted with candles to serve as lanterns at Halloween gatherings. The name "jack-o'-lantern" comes from an Irish tale of a man called Jack, who was notorious for his drunkenness and meanness. One Halloween night, Jack took a drink too many in the local pub, and his soul began to slip from his inebriated body. The Devil appeared at his side to claim his doomed spirit. But Jack was not yet ready to give up.

"Let's have one drink together before we go," he begged.

"Very well," replied his Satanic Majesty, "but you'll have to pay for it. I don't carry money with me."

"I have only sixpence," said Jack, "but you can change yourself into any shape, so they say. Change yourself into sixpence and then you can change back again when I've paid for the tot of grog."

This seemed a reasonable idea to the Devil, so he muttered an incantation and there he was on the bar counter, a shiny new sixpence. Jack snatched the coin and put it in his wallet which had a silver catch in the shape of a cross. The cross prevented the Devil from getting out. He muttered and cursed inside the wallet but he was unable to open the flap or get back into his own shape again.

"If you'll promise to let me alone for a year, I'll let you out," said Jack.

The Devil promised and Jack released him. Now Jack had in the back of his mind the notion that with a year's grace he could reform, take his pay home to his wife and children instead of spending it in the pub, go to Mass every Sunday, and put money in the poor box. Then the Devil couldn't take his soul. But as soon as Jack felt out of danger, he went back to his old mean ways.

The next Halloween, as Jack was anxiously hurrying home along a country road, the Devil was suddenly walking beside him, and Jack knew that he had come to claim his soul. As they walked they came to a tree hung with big red apples.

"Don't you want an apple?" suggested Jack.

"They're fine-looking apples, for sure," said the Devil, "but they all grow too high for picking."

"Stand on my shoulders," said Jack, "and then you can reach them."

So the Devil climbed up on Jack's shoulders, swung himself up to a branch of the tree and began to pick apples. Jack whipped out his pocketknife and cut the sign of the cross on the trunk of the tree, which made it impossible for the Devil to come down again.

"Let me out of this," cried the Devil, "and I won't claim your soul for ten years."

But Jack said, "I won't let you out of that tree until you promise me that you won't ever come after me any more."

The Devil, being desperate, gave his promise. Before the next Halloween, Jack's body just wore out and his soul had to go some place. He was turned away from heaven because he had been mean and stingy all his life, but when he got to the gates of hell, the Devil shouted, "Go away! You tricked me into promising that I'd not claim your soul. I must keep my word; you cannot enter hell."

"But where am I to go?"

"Back where you came from."

"How can I find my way in the windy dark?"

The Devil answered by throwing Jack a chunk of live coal from the hell furnace. Jack put it inside a turnip he was gnawing and with this "jack-o'-lantern" has been wandering the earth ever since, a lost soul with no place to go.

From his brimstone bed at the break of day,
A-walking the Devil has gone,
To visit his snug little farm of the earth,
And see how his stock goes on.
Over the hill and over the dale,
He walked, and over the plain:
And backward and forward he swished his long tail,
As a gentleman swishes his cane.

—ROBERT SOUTHEY, "The Devil's Walk"

The Witch in Europe

THE WITCH MOUNTED ON HER BROOM-
stick with her black cat perched behind her has become the symbol of Halloween. At gay Halloween
parties someone usually masquerades as a witch
with peaked hat and matted hair, the mask showing
nose and chin almost meeting over withered lips.
That is the stereotype of the witch, considered
comic nowadays.

But there was a time in our history when witchcraft was no laughing matter; when the best minds
of the church and the law devoted fervent efforts
toward stamping out the evil of these disciples of
Satan. The Bible says, "Thou shalt not suffer a
witch to live" (Exodus 22:18). These eight words,
plucked from their context and their background,
became a death sentence for many thousands.

To doubt the power of a witch was a form of
heresy. How could one truly have faith in God and

the saints if one denied the existence of the Devil and his cohorts? John Wesley said in 1768 that "giving up witchcraft is in effect giving up the Bible." Martin Luther, in his study in the castle of Wartburg, had personal struggles with the Devil and on one occasion threw an inkstand at his head. Furthermore it is not strange that people believed in witches, for the "witches" believed in themselves.

The witch is old in history. The Bible tells the story of the Witch of Endor, who was consulted by Saul before his battle with the Philistines. The Greeks and Romans had their witches, sibyls, and priestesses. However, these women were not regarded with revulsion or treated as criminals. The witches' lore was sought after; the old wise woman, with her charms, her fortune telling, and her herbs, was a recognized part of society. This is still true in many remote places where science and modern technology have not banished belief in magic. It was not until the Middle Ages, when Europe was in the throes of the struggle between Christianity and paganism, that the witch emerged as a sinister force.

After the fourth century, the spread of Christianity was rapid, but many of the pagan sects clung tenaciously to the old beliefs. Their temples were taken over and consecrated by the church, but the worshippers could not be changed by the sprinkling of holy water. The priests of Apollo, Diana, and Hecate, driven from the sacred groves, developed a new religion which became the witch cult.

However, as the church grew in power much of

its ritual seeped into the pagan worship. The souls in revolt pledged allegiance to Satan, who, as the anti-Christ, was a Christian concept. In mockery of the church they held the Black Mass, which was an obscene parody of divine worship. They used the nude body of a woman for an altar, recited the Lord's Prayer backwards and twisted the Ten Commandments so that "thou shalt" became "thou shalt not" and vice versa.

By the Middle Ages, the battle was joined between the church and the followers of the Prince of Darkness. Witches, warlocks, and sorcerers had to be weeded out if they were to be prevented from undermining the true church.

By the twelfth century, Christianity was strong enough to deal ruthlessly with its opponents. One of the agents of Pope Innocent VIII, who issued a papal bull in 1484 against witchcraft, boasted that he himself had supervised the execution of more than nine hundred witches and warlocks. These followers of Satan served their master with devotion and met their death unrepentant. The early church really had something to fear from this anti-Christ movement. Satan was not only the Prince of Evil, he was also the Prince of Pleasure. To many peasant folk, the excitement and ecstasy of the Witches' Sabbaths had more appeal than the droning monotony of the church services.

Although the satanic cults were a menace to the growing ascendancy of the church, the fear of witches persisted long after their real influence had died. The greatest witch persecutions took place in the sixteenth and seventeenth centuries, after witchcraft had become a sort of rubbish heap for out-worn creeds and superstitions.

Witchcraft of the third century and earlier was much less malevolent than that of the twelfth century; it continued to change in character until the Age of Reason in the eighteenth century drove away much of the superstitious fear which gave the witch her power. When the causes of illness and death are outside human comprehension, it is easy to believe that these afflictions are due to mysterious and evil machinations. It was science and the microscope which routed the witches' charms and images.

However, these beliefs die hard. The witch and the medicine man still practice their arts in primitive communities, and even in the United States accusations of witchcraft occasionally reach our courts. The New York *Herald Tribune*, on May 4, 1950, carried a story of a woman who had haled her neighbor into court on a charge of bewitchment. True, the judge threw the case out of court, but that it had got so far and was reported by the news services is noteworthy.

The question as to whether or not witches really had supernatural powers is still debated. Medieval clerics believed that the evil bewitchments were as real as the godly miracles of the saints. Modern authorities, for the most part, take the position that the witches were prey to hallucinations and auto-suggestion. However, no one who has lived among primitive peoples with strong beliefs in ghosts and

4. *The witches' Sabbath according to De Lancre; 1612.*

(Courtesy of the New York Public Library)

5. *An execution of witches in England.*

(Courtesy of the New York Public Library)

6. *Contract drawn up between the devil and Urbain Grandier.*

Urbain Grandier, a priest, appeared in Loudun, France, in the 1620's and was considered the cause of bewitching the nuns of the convent. Bibliothèque Nationale, Paris.

(Courtesy of the New York Public Library)

spirits can deny that there are forces in operation which cannot be explained by modern science.

Be that as it may, the witches undoubtedly believed in their own powers and in the sinful bond which they made with the Prince of Darkness. Their organization was a closed one with a secret and devoted membership. The local witch congregations and meetings were called "covens." This referred to a company of twelve, with the Devil, or his agent, as the thirteenth—in impious imitation of Christ and the twelve disciples. The Devil, or master of ceremonies, appeared in a mask and his identity was usually unknown to the rest of the assemblage, who doubtless believed him an emissary straight from hell. Evil men sometimes made use of this custom to lure excitable women to these meetings and lead them into evil ways.

The novice who wished to be initiated into the mysteries of witchcraft had to be recommended and introduced by other witches. When her application had been favorably passed upon, she would be summoned to appear before the assembled coven. There she must formally renounce adherence to any other religion and swear allegiance to the Devil, represented by the master of ceremonies. This masked man would place one hand on the crown of the candidate's head and the other on the sole of her foot. He would then declare that from that time forward all that was betwixt his two hands— body and soul—was at the Devil's service. The new witch was then baptized with a new name and admonished to keep the witches' commandment: to do as much harm as possible and never to reveal any of the witches' secrets.

The Witches' Sabbaths were the large, general meetings held at night at which many covens assembled. The principal Sabbaths were held at the four quarters of the year. The most important of these were May Eve (April 30), called Roodmas in England and Walpurgis Night in Germany, and Halloween. Between these came Candlemas (February 2) and the Gule of August (August 1), called Lammas in Britain. It was said that on the first Monday after each of these festivals anyone who went to a hill overlooking the town and watched the smoke rising from the morning fires could pick out the houses where witches dwelt. The smoke from a witch's chimney traveled against the wind rather than with it, as smoke from honest fires does.

The Sabbaths were scenes of feasting and revelry. Witches, warlocks, and devils danced in a ring. (This is reminiscent of the rings worn by fairy feet, which Irish peasants report from the forest glades.) There are many contemporary descriptions of these revels. The dance was usually performed by couples, back to back with arms linked. They would caper around the circle in this strange position and at intervals one or another of the team would bend forward carrying his partner, legs kicking in air, on his back. This dance must have presented a weird spectacle of thrashing limbs and diabolic capers.

7. *Witches making their magic unguent. From a wood-cut of the 15th century, Ulrich Molitor.*

(Courtesy of the New York Public Library)

Many witches who reported attending Sabbaths at considerable distances from their homes claimed that they went by air on a broomstick. In order for them to accomplish this feat, a special ointment had to be brewed. With this, the witch anointed herself and her broomstick. Reginald Scot, in his *Discoverie of Witchcraft* (1584), gives the following recipe for witch ointment:

The fat of young children, and seethe with water in a brazen vessel, reserving the thickest of that which remaineth boiled at the bottom, which they lay up and keep until occasion serveth to use it. They put hereunto Eleoselinum, Aconite, belladonna, soote, and

Solan Somniferum. They mix all these together, and then rub all parts of their bodies exceedingly till they look red and be very hot, so as the pores may be opened and their flesh soluble and loose. They join herewithal fat or oil that the force of the ointment may pierce inwards and so be more effectual. By this means on a moonlight night, they seem to be carried in the air to feastings, singings, dancing, kissings, and embracing and other acts.

It is small wonder that the witches, well permeated with this concoction, could believe that they were soaring over the housetops to join the lurid merrymaking. Most of the drugs in the witches' pharmacopoeia were of a sort known to produce vascular excitement and hallucinations: mandrake, poppy, belladonna, foxglove, henbane, deadly nightshade, and Indian hemp.

The mandrake was the most powerful and mysterious of these deadly herbs. Wine made from this root produced deep sleep and lurid dreams. It was believed that the mandrake shrieked and moaned when it was pulled from the ground and that he who drew it would go mad or die.

And shrieks like mandrakes torn out of the earth
That living mortals hearing them run mad.
    —WILLIAM SHAKESPEARE, *Romeo and Juliet*

The only safe way to gather mandrake roots was to go out on a dark night with a black dog. One of the dog's legs was firmly tied to the plant by a stout cord; in the animal's struggles to free himself, the plant was uprooted. It was wise to carry a horn on these occasions, so that, as the root came out, one could toot loudly and therefore be spared the maddening shrieks of the mandrake.

The novice was instructed in the use of all these drugs and ointments. One of the tools of the craft which she must learn to make (the assembling of the ingredients for which took considerable doing) was the witch candle. This was made from the fat of an unbaptized baby; hair from the head of a hanged man; the finger of a murderer, grave-robbed; and a few other lurid objects. But having collected these things and made the candle, the witch could laugh at locksmiths. To gain entry to any house, the witch had only to hold her lighted candle to the door and the stoutest lock would fly open.

Although the witch was expert at brewing poisons, the main method of injuring an enemy was to make a doll or puppet in his image. This was more effective if some of the victim's hair cuttings or nail parings could be obtained. The images were of wax, lead, or wood. When the doll was held over the fire so that the heat melted or distorted part of its body, the corresponding section of the human counterpart would waste away or be afflicted with disease. Pins were also stuck into these images, whereupon the bewitched person would feel great pain in the corresponding region of his anatomy.

This method of afflicting enemies was widespread and is still practiced by medicine men in primitive tribes. At a charity bazaar held in London in 1901 toward the close of the Boer War, an image of Stephanus Kruger, the Boer president, was

8. Witches bringing a shower of rain. Ulrich Molitor,
De Laniis et phitonicis mulieribus. *Constance, 1489.*

(Courtesy of the New York Public Library)

exhibited. On payment of sixpence, visitors were
provided with long pins and permitted to pierce
the image three times in the location of their choice.
This proved a highly profitable attraction at the
bazaar. Although the English probably intended it
as a joke, there was enough credulity in the game
to give the players solid satisfaction. No doubt if a
similar money-raising scheme had been tried with
an image of Hitler during the Second World War,
many takers could have been found.

In 1940 a New York doctor telephoned one of
the authors of this book to ask his advice on a puz-
zling case. A patient had come to the hospital in a

hysterical condition saying that he had been bewitched and would die within forty-eight hours. The doctor scoffed at this, but the man failed rapidly, although no medical reason for his illness could be found. The symptoms were like those of severe shock. The doctor called upon an anthropologist because he knew that he had had experience with witchcraft murders among primitives. But it was too late. The patient's temperature, blood pressure, and heartbeat became so low that he finally died. An autopsy showed no injury or disease of any of the organs. The only way to have saved him would have been to have convinced him that the spell had been broken by a countermagic.

The efficacy of all magic practices is based very largely upon the power of suggestion. If one believes in the effectiveness of magic and knows that a charm is being worked against him, he is very likely to experience the symptoms which the magic is designed to produce.

THE CAT!

Who pads through the wood
   Where cypresses grow,
When the sun goes down
   And night-winds blow?
      The cat!

Who slinks through the cave
   In the side of the hill
Where black bats swoop
   From a cobwebbed sill?
      The cat!

Who purrs by the grave
   Of unshriven dead,
While witches dance
   And ghouls are fed?
      The cat! . . . SKAT!!!

—JOSEPH PAYNE BRENNAN

6

The Witch Cat

CAT-LOVERS ARE ADVISED TO SKIP this chapter. The Halloween cat is not a pretty pussy purring on the hearthrug but a baleful black feline which consorts with witches and demons.

This concept of the cat as a sinister and magical animal goes back to ancient times. The Egyptians worshipped the cat as a deity. In the legends of Greece and Rome, a woman who had been changed into a cat was chosen as priestess by Hecate, the goddess of sorcery and the patron of witches.

In classical times the cat fared rather well as a feared but respected beast. But during the witch persecutions, the cats were tortured and killed along with their mistresses. Probably the cat was associated with the witch because cats are the frequent companions of strange, lonely old women who are likely to be regarded as witches. Then, too, there is something sinister in the stealthy grace, the green glare, and the demonic whiskers. Both dogs and cats are widely credited with extrasensory perceptions; but dogs in the presence of the supernatural are said to bristle or slink away, whereas cats are unperturbed by ghosts or haunted houses.

Witches and devils are believed not only to use cats as familiars, or mascots, but to change themselves into cats at will. Since one could never be sure whether a cat was an innocent pussy or a witch in disguise, all cats were suspect. It was on this principle that cats were thrown into the fire on the nights of the great witch meetings. It was highly probable that the cat was either itself a witch or was preparing to attend the Sabbath riding on the broomstick behind its mistress. To burn the cat therefore was a warning to other witches. In Ireland, black cats were thrown into the Halloween fires. In Europe, they were burned on May Eve.

In Ireland, the usual salutation on entering a cottage was "God save all here, barring the cat." Cats were connected with the devil and could not receive a blessing. The Irish also believed that, if a man begins a journey and encounters a cat which stares him full in the face, he had best turn around and go home, for a witch is in his path and his journey will turn out badly. The notion that it is bad luck to have a black cat cross one's path is a widespread superstition. Many people today will turn back or go around the block rather than cross the path of a black cat.

The fear of cats as being witches in disguise is illustrated in the famous trial of Bartie Paterson in

England in 1607. Her accuser testified in court that Bartie had bewitched her and then, in the form of a cat, had capered and yowled in the company of other felines all night long in her victim's back yard. The judge accepted this testimony as conclusive evidence of witchcraft and Bartie was hanged.

All witches were thought to have familiars who did their bidding and helped them in their nefarious mischief. J. W. Wickwar, in *Witchcraft and the Black Art*, says that the cat, the dog, the many-teated sow, and the goat were chosen as familiars because they are unusually fecund animals. The Devil encouraged witches to have prolific progeny so that they might outnumber and smother the Christians. This was no doubt a later rationalization of the inclusion in the witch cults of many features of the pre-Christian fertility cults. Witch mothers were supposed to dedicate their offspring to Satan at birth and to instruct them in magic lore. It was because of this practice that children were frequently arrested as witches and sometimes tortured and executed. It was reasoned that, if the mother was a witch, the child had also been instructed in the fiendish lore.

Witches were encouraged to act as midwives, so that they could pledge the newborn children to Satan before they could be baptized. Since the fat of unbaptized infants was a basic ingredient in the witch pharmacopoeia, witches were a menace to newborn infants, in any case.

Although other animals were used as familiars, it was the black cat which was the witch's most frequent companion and therefore the symbol of Halloween. The superstitions about cats are legion. In Ireland there was a belief that one could make from a special bone of a black cat a charm which would make one invisible. The procedure was as follows: A black cat was boiled alive and the bones separated and cleaned. Then the magician stood in front of a mirror and put the bones one at a time into his mouth, meanwhile watching his reflection. When he came to a bone which failed to reflect in the mirror, this was the magic article from which the charm of invisibility could be made.

The blood of a black cat also had magical properties. Laid on an open wound with a raven's feather, it healed the wound immediately.

The liver of a black cat, dried and brewed with tea in a black pot, was considered a powerful love charm. A girl had merely to invite her young man to tea and serve him some made in this way, and he was certain to look at her thenceforth with a gleam in his eye.

Cats also had magical control of weather. The seafaring Scots believed that by burying a cat alive one could cause a breeze to spring up in the direction in which the cat's head faced. By shutting a cat in the cupboard one could create unfavorable winds for ships trying to reach port, thereby detaining unwelcome arrivals.

A famous cat story told in various versions in northern England concerns a gentleman who was sitting one night before his fire calmly reading a book when he heard a scuttling in the chimney. A cat appeared in the fireplace, leaped across the logs

into the room, and called out, "Tell Dildrum Doldrum's dead," and then disappeared up the chimney
again. The gentleman, much startled by this occur-
rence, called to his wife, who came into the room
with the family cat at her heels. The husband told
her what had happened, whereupon the cat, which
up to now had seemed a well-behaved pet, ex-
claimed, "So Doldrum is dead," leaped across the
fire and up the chimney, and he was never seen
again. The interpretation of this tale is that Doldrum was king of Catland and Dildrum, who had
been living quietly as a housecat in a respectable
family, was the next heir.

John Gregorson Campbell recounts a tale told in
Scotland of an English doctor who came to the
highlands for the hunting season. He was sitting
before the fire in his bothy, or hut, one evening
after a day's sport when a cat walked in through
the open door. The dogs growled and bristled but
did not move. The cat sat down with its back to
the fire and began to swell until it was as large as a
yearling calf. The dogs pretended not to notice.
The doctor pulled a silver button from his coat
(only a silver bullet is effective against a witch),
put it in his gun, and fired it at the cat, which fled
yowling. The next morning, a windy, rainy day
(when a cat sits with its back to the fire, it always
raises a storm), a farmer came to the cabin door to
ask the doctor to call on his sick wife. When the
doctor examined the woman, he found a wound in
her chest. He cleaned it and extracted from her
right breast his own silver button.

Cats were intimately associated with one of the witches' most dangerous arts—raising tempests at sea. This is the basis of the belief that if one has a cat on board the ship cannot be wrecked by witchcraft, since the animal acts as a countercharm. The approved method of causing tempests was to baptize a cat in a mock ceremony, then fasten to the luckless animal some portion of human anatomy and throw the grisly combination into the sea.

The most famous case of this sort of magic was that of the witches of Norway and Scotland versus James VI of Scotland, later James I of England. The monarch had chosen as his bride the Dano-Norwegian princess Ann, daughter of Frederick II. The witches of both Norway and Scotland disapproved of the match. When the bride, in the royal ship with an escort of eleven other vessels, set sail from Norway for Scotland to meet the groom, the witches caused a charmed cat with a human leg attached to be thrown into the sea. The resulting tempests were so severe that the bridal fleet had to return to Norway.

King James, in a fury of impatience, then set sail for Norway to fetch his bride himself. The news spurred the witches to renewed deviltry. This time they tossed into the sea a cat with dead men's knucklebones tied to its four paws. To make certain that the King did not reach his destination, the Devil arranged a meeting with witches from both countries on the sea on Halloween night, when the King's fleet would be halfway across the North Sea. The sorceresses set out from both coasts in sieves (the favorite barks of witches) and met the

Devil at the appointed spot. It is recorded that they encountered a ship named "Grace of God," boarded her, feasted on all the ship's stores, and then whipped up a tempest which foundered the ship and drowned all those aboard, so that there were no survivors to confirm this story.

After the sinking of the "Grace of God," more than a hundred witches sailed back to Scotland in their sieves and held a great revel at the church in North Berwick, where, after opening the lock with a witch candle, they danced around the pulpit, rifled graves and vaults, and amused themselves greatly. So pious was the King, however, that the Devil's charms were powerless against him and he reached Norway safely. Many witches paid with their lives for this attempt. The account of the enchantments briefly sketched above (there are reams of testimony on this affair) was taken from the "confessions" of the witches involved.

Some only for not being drown'd,
And some for sitting above ground
Whole nights and days upon their breeches
And feeling pain, were hanged for witches.

—SAMUEL BUTLER, "Hudibras"

7

"Witch Finder General"

IN THE SUPERSTITION-RIDDEN MIDDLE Ages, it was understandable that there should be dread of witches. The witch huntings of the seventeenth century, however, had a different character. They had a religious excuse: the warnings of the Bible and the sanction of the church, but there was also a political and emotional character to the persecutions which was not found in the earlier day. At times of political tension or unrest, injustice and hysteria are likely to be present. And every bigot and zealous informer makes use of this atmosphere for his own purposes. We cannot be too scornful of the excesses of former times, for at times of fear and chaos we do our own witch hunting.

People were still ruled by superstition in the seventeenth century, but there were many who saw in witch persecutions an opportunity to advance themselves by battening on the public fantasies. Chief among these was a lawyer named Matthew Hopkins, who set himself up as "Witch Finder General," a self-conferred title. Professing to be an expert in the discovery of witches, he traveled through the counties of southern England, exacting a substantial sum from each town which he helped to rid of its witches. He claimed to be in possession of a notebook, which he had tricked the Devil into giving him, containing the names of many witches who had signed the Devil's pact. He also managed to standardize the various tests which were used to determine guilt at witch trials. Hopkins' tests continued to be used long after the outraged citizenry turned on him at last and gave him a taste of his own medicine.

In one of the Hopkins' tests the victim was taken to an old barn and forced to strip naked and sit cross-legged on a stool or table placed in the center of the building. Hopkins and his assistants would then go over the prisoner with long pins made especially "to find the mark." This mark was supposed to be the spot where the Devil had put his seal. It was insensible to all feeling and did not bleed. To find such a spot on the body was definite proof that the person was in league with the Devil.

As soon as the victims understood the meaning of this torture, they would of course cry out each time the pin went in. Hopkins took care of this by inventing a pricking instrument, made on the telescopic principle, which could be manipulated so that sometimes the pin went in and sometimes it did not. If the terrified victim screamed when the pin did not touch her body, it was almost as great a count against her as if she had not screamed when it did. It saved the victim some pain but increased the tension of the examination.

The mark having been found, as it usually was, it was believed that an imp, or succubus, would come to suck at it. A guard was assigned to watch through an aperture for the imp to come. The guard seldom failed to report such a phenomenon, since as soon as it was reported he could doze off comfortably.

Another of Hopkins' tests consisted of "swimming the witch." The idea was that water, being a pure element, will reject an evil, unbaptized person, so that witches do not sink. In this ordeal by water, the victim was taken to a pond. Here her two thumbs were tied with cord to her two great toes. She was then placed in a sheet which was loosely tied by the four corners by a cord with a long end. The bundle was placed at the edge of the pond. Someone at the other side of the pond would pull the bundle across by the cord. If it floated, as it usually did, being full of air as well as witch, the verdict was "guilty." If by some chance the bundle became soggy and sank before it reached the opposite edge of the pond but the witch failed to drown, her innocence was not necessarily proved. She was usually tortured into a confession. Few ever escaped the ban of Hopkins once he had made his charges.

At the end of three years of this cruelty, the people revolted against it. An obscure clergyman named Gaule, living in the town of Stoughton, in

Huntingdon, began preaching and writing against the cruelties of witch hunting in general and Hopkins in particular. This was a courageous thing to do, for Hopkins was almost sure to bring charges of witchcraft against anyone who opposed him— a practice which was one of the secrets of his success. When Hopkins attempted to convince the dignitaries of Stoughton that they were in dire need of his services, these functionaries, to their everlasting credit, turned a cold shoulder and refused to let him and his assistants come to their town.

This broke Hopkins' power. Reluctant to lose such a profitable business, he began to advertise with leaflets distributed to one town after another. But the tide had turned. Hopkins was seized, accused of wizardry, and subjected to his own "ordeal by water." He failed to sink and was hanged on the gallows in 1677.

This was not the end of witch hunting in England, however. Public interest in the dismal business was kept alive by news sheets, street ballads, and notorious witch tracts, much as public hysteria is whipped up by yellow journalism today. Many of these witch tracts are still in existence and bring high prices from collectors. The following tract is in the possession of J. W. Wickwar and appears in his book *Witchcraft and the Black Art:*

"*Witch Finder General*"

THE
Northamptonshire Witches

Being a true and faithful ACCOUNT of the Births, Educations, Lives, and Conversations,

OF
Ellinor Shaw, and *Mary Phillips*
(The two notorious Witches)
That were Executed at *Northampton* on *Saturday*, March the 17th, 1705, for bewitching a Woman and two Children to death. &c.

CONTAINING

The manner and occasion of their turning Witches, the League they made with the Devil, and the strange Discourse they had with him; As also the particulars of their amazing Pranks and remarkable Actions, both before and after their Apprehension, and how they bewitched several Persons to Death, besides abundance of all sorts of Cattle, even to the ruin of many Families, with their full Confession to the Minister, and last Dying Speeches at the place of Execution, the like never before heard of.

Communicated in a Letter last Post, from Mr. *Ralph Davis of Northampton,* to Mr. William Simons, Merchantt in *London.*

Licensed according to Order.
London, Printed for F. Thorn, near Fleet-street, 1705

THE
Northamptonshire Witches.
THE
Birth and Education, Lives, and Conversations,
of Ellinor Shaw, and Mary Phillips, &c.

Sir,

According to my Promise in my last, I have sent you here Inclosed a faithful Account of the Lives, and Conversations of the two notorious Witches, that were Executed on the Northside of our Town on Saturday the 17th instant, and indeed considering the extraordinary Methods these wicked Women used to accomplish their Diabolical Art; I think it may merit your Reception, and the more, since I understand you have a Frind near Fleet-street, who being a Printer, may make use of it in order to oblige the Publick; which take as followeth, viz.

To proceed in order, I shall first begin with Ellinor Shaw (as being the most notorious of the two) who was Born at Cotterstock, within a small Mile of Oundle in Northamptonshire, of very obscure Parents, who not willing, or at least not able to give their Daughter any manner of Education; she was left to shift for her self at the age of 14 years, at which time she got acquainted with a Partener in Wickedness, one Mary Phillips, Born at Oundle aforesaid, with whom she held a frindly Correspondence for several Years together, and Work'd very hard in a seeming honest way for a Livelihood; but when she arriv'd to the age of 21 she began to be a very wicked Person talk'd of not only in the town of Cotterstock where she was Born, but at Oundle, Glapthorn, Benefield, Southwick, and several Parts adjacent, and that as well by Children of four or five Years of age, as Persons of riper Years; so that by degrees her Name became so famous,

or rather infamous, that she could hardly peep out of
her Door, but the Children would point at her in a
Scoffing manner, saying, There goes a Witch, there's
Nell the Strumpet, &c. which repeated Disgrace, agra-
vated her Passion to such a degree, that she Swore she
would be revenged on her Enemies, tho she pawn'd
her Soul for the Purchase. To Mary Phillips her Partener in Knitting, who was as bad as her self in the Vices
aforesaid she then communicated her Thoughts, re-
lating to a Contract with the Devil. . . . In fine, as
these two agreed in their Wickedness, to go Hand in
Hand to the Devil together for Company; but out of
a kind of Civility, he sav'd them that Trouble for he
immediately waited upon 'em to obtain his Booty, on
Saturday the 12th of February 1704, about 12 a Clock
at Night (according to their own Confessions) ap-
pearing in the shape of a black tall Man, at whose approach they were very much startled at first, but taking Ellinor Shaw by the Hand he spoke thus, says he,
be not afraid for having power given me to bestow it
on whom I please, I do assure you, that if you will
pawn your Souls to me for only a Year and two
Months, I will for all that time assist you in whatever
you desire: Upon which he produced a little piece of
Parchment, on which by their Consents (having
prick't their Fingers ends) he wrote the Infernal Cov-
enant in their own Blood, which they signed with their
own Hands, after which he told them they were now
as substantial Witches as any were in the World, and
that they had power by the assistance of the Imps,
that he would send them to do what Mischief they
pleased.

I shall not trouble you with what is already mention'd in the Tryals of these two Persons, because it
is in Print by your Friend already, but only instance
what was omitted in that, as not having room here to

contain it altogether; but as to their general Confessions after their Condemnations take as followeth.

The Day before they were Executed Mr. Danks the Minister visited them in Prison; in order if possible to bring them to a State of Repentance, but seeing all pious Discourse prov'd inefectual; he desired them to tell him what mischeivous Pranks they had Play'd, and what private Conference they had with the Devil, from time to time, since they had made that fatal Bargain with him: To which Ellinor Shaw with the Consent of the other, told him, that the Devil in the Shape of a Tall black Man appear'd several times to them, and at every Visit would present them with new Imps, some of a Red Colour others of a Dun and the third of a black Colour, and that these infernal Imps did Nightly visit each of them; and that by the assistance of these Animals they often Kill'd Men, Women, and Children, to the great surprise of all the Towns thereabouts; she further adding that it was all the Delight they had to be doing such wicked Actions, and that they had Kil'd by their Inchantments, and Witchcraft in the space of nine Months time 15 Children, eight Men, and six Women, tho' none was suspected of being Bewitch'd but those two Children and the Woman that they Dy'd for; and that they had Bewitch'd to Death in the same Space of Time 40 Hoggs of several poor People, besides 100 Sheep, 18 Horses, and 30 Cows, even to the utter Ruin of several Families: As to their particular Intreagues and waggish Tricks, I have not Room to enumerate they are so many, only some remarkable Feats they did in Prison, which was thus, viz. one Day Mr. Laxon and his Wife coming by the Prison, had the Curiosity to look through the Grates, and seeing Ellinor Shaw, told her, that now the Devil had left her in the Lurch as he had done the rest of his Servants; upon which the said Ellinor,

was observ'd to Mutter strangely to her-self in an unknown Language for about two Minutes, at the end
of which Mr. Laxon's Wifes Cloaths were all turn'd
over her Head, Smock and all in a most strange manner, and stood so for some time at which the said Ellinor having Laughed Heartily. The Keeper of the
Prison, having one Day Threatned them with Irons,
they by their Spells caused him to Dance almost an
Hour in the yard, to the Amazment of the Prison,
nay, such Pranks, were Play'd by them during their
Confinement, that no one durst give them an ill Word,
insomuch that their Execution was the more hastened
in the regard of their frequent Disturbances, and great
Mischief they did in several places of the Town, not-
withstanding their Imprisonment:

They were so hardened in their Wickedness that
Publickly boasted that their Master, (meaning the
Devil) would not suffer them to be Executed, but on
Saturday Morning being the 17th Instant they were
carried to the Gallows on the North-side of the Town
whither numerous Crowd's of People went to see
them Die, and being come to the place of Execution,
the Minister repeated his former pious Endeavours, to
bring them to a sence of their Sins, but to as little purpose as before; for instead of calling on God for
Mercy, nothing was heard from them but very bad
language: However a little before they were ty'd up,
at the request of the Minister, Ellinor Shaw confessed not only the Crime for which she Dyed, but
openly declared before them all how she first became
a Witch, as did also Mary Phillips; and being desired
to say their Prayers, they both set up a very loud
Laughter, calling for the Devil to come and help
them in such a Blasphemous manner, as is not fit to
Mention; so that the Sherif seeing their presumptious
Impenitence, caused them to be Executed with all the

Expedition possible; even while they were raving, and as they liv'd the Devils true Factors, so they resolutely Dyed in his Service, to the Terror all People who were eye Witnesses of their dreadful and amazing Exits.

So that being Hang'd till they were almost Dead, the Fire was put to the Straw, Faggots, and other Combustable matter, till they were Burnt to Ashes. Thus Liv'd and thus Dyed, two of the most notorious and presumptious Witches, that ever were known in this Age.

I am Sir,
Your Humble Servant
RALPH DAVIS.

Northampton, March 18th 1705

Then she steals forth to make ewes
Cast their lambs, swine eat their farrow,
And housewives' tun not work, nor the milk churn!
Writhe children's wrists and suck their breath in sleep,
Get vials of their blood! and where the sea
Casts up his slimy ooze, search for a weed
To open locks with, and to rivet charms
Planted about her in the wicket feat
Of all her mischiefs, which are manifold.

—BEN JONSON

Witchcraft in New England

ALTHOUGH THE SETTLERS OF THIS country looked upon the red men as poor benighted heathen full of superstition, there were shreds of paganism still clinging even to the rigid doctrine of the Pilgrims and Puritans. Belief in witchcraft crossed the ocean with them. It was rampant in England at the time. It is estimated that 40,000 witches were put to death in England during the lifetime of John Alden. Such fancies may seem incompatible with the stern Puritan conscience, but one must remember that the Calvinists regarded Satan as a powerful and ever-present force. The sermons of the Puritan preachers reeked of brimstone and grim warnings against the wiles of the devil. And where Satan is, his servants, the witches, warlocks, and imps, are active also.

The Pilgrims of the Plymouth settlement, although witchcraft was a capital offense in their lawbooks, showed remarkable common sense in this matter, considering the superstitions of the day. A case is recorded in which Dinah Sylvester accused the wife of William Holmes, one of Miles Standish's lieutenants, of being a witch. Dinah testified in court that the woman had changed herself into a bear and had attacked her. John Howland, the presiding magistrate, put an end to such charges by fining Dinah five pounds and ordering her to be whipped. If the officials of Salem in 1692 had shown similar common sense, much misery would have been averted.

The first execution for witchcraft in New England took place in Boston in 1648, and the colony of Connecticut hanged a witch in 1650. But it was in the village of Salem in the winter of 1692 that witch hunting really reached alarming heights in New England. Compared to the European massacres, this was a modest affair, since only twenty people lost their lives. The Salem case is unique in that many of the judges and witnesses later confessed and repented of their crimes against innocent people. The families of the executed witches received recompense in many cases, something most unusual in the history of witchcraft. Despite the bigotry and tension which produced this reign of terror, the Puritans were essentially a sound and just people. When they recovered from the fever, they had the grace and honesty to repent.

Another unique feature of the Salem case is that it was fomented and directed by children. Probably never before have two children, one nine and the other eleven, been the cause of so much sorrow and misery.

It all began in the kitchen of the Reverend Samuel Parris, minister of Salem, now the town of Danvers, Massachusetts. There were two children in the household: Betty, a quiet, biddable little girl of nine, and her cousin, Abigail Williams, aged eleven. Abigail was the sort of child who nowadays would have been out playing baseball with the neighborhood boys, tearing around the block on roller skates, and shinnying up trees. Pilgrim children, however, did not behave that way. Abigail, dressed like a prim little matron in long gown, apron, and kerchief, had to sit quietly and work at her knitting. She did not find it so bad in the summer, when the children could get away to the woods and pick berries and flowers or could carry lunches to the men in the fields. But in the long, cold winters there was nothing for them to do. They seldom went out except to go to Sunday meeting, where they sat on hard benches and heard about the horrors of hell.

Mrs. Parris was busy with her good works as the wife of the pastor and left the children to the care of Tituba, a slave whom the Parrises had brought from Barbados. Tituba, half Carib and half Negro, eased her homesickness by talking to the children about the colorful, languorous life of her native islands. She scorned the grim Puritan creed and yearned for the land where voodoo and charms and spells were an accepted part of a wise woman's lore. It is no wonder that the two bored, neglected little girls haunted the kitchen; it is no wonder either that they told their friends about these exciting things. Soon some of the older girls in the neighborhood began dropping in at the Parris kitchen, particularly when they were sure that the mistress of the house was out on her errands of mercy and that the pastor was working on his sermons in the study.

Just what went on in the Parris kitchen no one really knows. Fortunetelling, undoubtedly. Some of the girls were old enough to be curious about their future husbands and all were at an age where the future beckons, full of unsounded mystery. Apparently they held séances also, during which Tituba called on the spirits of the dead, to the delight and horror of the children.

Abigail was having the time of her life, but Betty, who was a good child, strictly raised, knew that this was wrong; that these things were of the Devil and not of God. She was too much under Abigail's dominance to tattle to her parents, but the situation preyed upon her nine-year-old mind. She began to have strange spells during which she would sit, her sewing in her hands, her eyes glazed and blank. When she was spoken to, she would shriek or babble. She cried out during family prayers or even at church when the Devil was mentioned. Abigail, observing the attention and sympathy which Betty was receiving, became afflicted also. She made hoarse noises and ran around the room on all fours, like a dog. She too began to shriek during prayers. This was undoubtedly the way Abigail had always wanted to behave, but she had never before dared. The doctor was sum-

9. *Witches confessing the names of their imps and familiars. From an old print.*

(Courtesy of the New York Public Library)

10.   Witch trial at Salem Village.

(Courtesy of the Bettmann Archive, New York)

11.   Tituba and the children.

(Courtesy of the New York Public Library)

moned, but his pills and ointments were of no avail. "The children are bewitched," he said.

As this electrifying news spread through the village, some of the other girls who had been attending séances in Tituba's kitchen began to exhibit curious symptoms also—in particular, Ann Putnam, a frail, precocious twelve-year-old. She went into such convulsions and twitchings that her life was frequently despaired of and neighbors came from miles around to help her sorrowing mother—and also to see the exciting phenomenon. In spite of the violence of these attacks, the girls always emerged from them refreshed and with good appetite.

The next step, of course, was to discover who was responsible for this tormenting of innocents. But when asked, "Who torments you?" the girls would only shake their heads and go into further convulsions. Tituba, who was devoted to her charges, was as worried as the parents about the state of the children. In hope of curing them by the only means she knew, she concocted a charm to drive away the devils. She mixed rye meal with the urine of the two girls and baked the mixture in the ashes while mumbling incantations over it. This witch cake was then fed to the dog. The idea was that the demons would then turn their attentions to the beast and leave the children alone. The dog, unused to such pleasant attentions in this grim society, ate the cake with relish, but the situation remained unchanged; that is, it was unchanged until news of the witch cake permeated from the kitchen to the minister's study. Reverend Parris, horrified to learn that witch's devilment was going on under his own roof demanded of the children if it was Tituba who had bewitched them. They went off into wild delirium, probably prompted by terror at being found out, but this was taken as proof of Tituba's guilt.

Meanwhile two other women had been named by some of the other sufferers. One was Sarah Good, an old vagrant who, with her matted hair, leathery face, and evil-smelling pipe, was the perfect stereotype of the witch. The other was Sarah Osburne, a well-to-do matron, about whom there had been some gossip because she had lived with her hired man for some time before getting the sanction of the minister for the union. Sarah, annoyed with this talk, had been staying away from meeting.

This ill-assorted trio was charged with causing the torments of the girls. Tituba had been exhaustively questioned by Reverend Parris. When she had tried to tell him the truth, he refused to believe anything against the children, claiming that she was inventing the stories of what went on in the kitchen in a vile attempt to blame innocent little ones. He took a whip to her, and the terrified slave changed her story into one more acceptable to her white master.

Tuesday, March 1, 1692, was the date set for the preliminary hearings. So large a crowd assembled that Deacon Ingersoll's chamber, which usually served as a courtroom, was wholly inadequate and the session had to be held in the meetinghouse.

John Hathorn and Jonathan Corwin conducted the proceedings. Sarah Good was the first witch to come before the court. She denied all charges. When asked why she did not come to meeting, she replied, "For want of clothes!" Some of the villagers testified that when she had come to their houses begging and been refused she had gone off muttering imprecations and that after this their cows had died. Sarah claimed that she was merely muttering the Commandments. However, when asked to recite the Commandments, she was entirely at a loss. She was contemptuously dismissed and Sarah Osburne was summoned.

Sarah Osburne was ill and had to be supported to the stand. She testified that she was "more like to be bewitched than that she should be a witch," and told a rambling story of a black thing that pinched her and pulled her hair.

Then Tituba was brought in. The girls, who were lined up in a place of honor in the courtroom, went into paroxysms at sight of her. However, when Tituba's testimony began, there was an awed silence in the courtroom, children and adults alike listening with rapt attention. Tituba, having discovered that the truth did her no good, gave her primitive imagination full rein and told the court what they wanted to hear.

As a slave, she had learned to look for cues and adapt her responses to the temper of the whites. With this ability and her own fertile invention, Tituba put on a performance which enraptured her audience. It had been a long, dull winter, with no books, no radios, no motion pictures to break the monotony; this session was better than a carnival for the bored villagers.

For three days, Tituba had all the townsfolk hanging on her words—words which came very near to hanging her. She drew satisfaction, however, from her brief period of glory. Her "confession" grew more colorful as she gained confidence. Finding that the adults responded to her tales with as much awe as did the little girls in the kitchen, she drew upon all her knowledge of voodoo and spirit lore, spicing it with extravagant fancyings. She told of the tall black man who came and tempted her with "pretty things." She told of red cats and red rats.

She said that Sarah Good and Sarah Osburne appeared at her bedside and forced her to pinch the children and poke them with knives. She said she had attended Witches' Sabbaths flying through the air on a broom in company with the tall man, a hog, and two cats. The man had made her sign a book in which there were other names, nine in all; but the only names Tituba remembered were those of Sarah Good and Sarah Osburne. The fact that Tituba could neither read nor write apparently made this startling testimony no less valid. These three, then, were not all. There were other witches to be ferreted out.

Events seemed to prove that this was indeed the case, for after the three witches were condemned and locked up the children were no better; in fact, more girls and even a few boys were taken with the dreadful seizures. The contagious hysteria of teenagers is now a recognized phenomenon. When the bobby-soxers screamed and swooned at the Paramount Theatre, no one accused Frank Sinatra of being a warlock who had bewitched them. The Puritan adolescents were accustomed to a repression which even the strictest parents could not enforce today. The bewitched state of the "Salem wenches" brought them freedom and attention such as no child had heretofore enjoyed in this stern society. It also provided them with a marvelous opportunity to get back at every grown-up who had ever snubbed or humiliated them. They had merely to go into a convulsion and say that Rebecca Nurse or Martha Crosly was choking them and the good wife would be dragged to court. How can anyone prove that she is not a witch?

Rebecca Nurse was seventy-one years old and all her life had been a model of what a Puritan woman should be. She was never absent from meeting. She had raised four sons and four daughters and at the time of the witch trials also had three sons-in-law and four daughters-in-law. All her children were pious and respectable and all remained loyal and devoted to her during her disgrace. Seventy-one years of devotion and industry availed nothing when Ann Putnam shrieked, "No, no, I will not sign, take the awful book away," and explained that Rebecca Nurse was tormenting her in an attempt to make her sign the Devil's book. Rebecca Nurse went to the gallows along with the jades and crones who had likewise been accused. The weather-beaten house from which the sick old woman was dragged still stands in a meadow near Danvers. Behind it is the family burying ground, where her sorrowing children secretly buried her body.

Rebecca Nurse was the oldest of the witches. Poor little Dorcas Good, aged five, was the youngest. She was suspected because her mother was a witch and witches were known to pass on their evil lore to their offspring. Dorcas was not executed, but the months she spent in jail at that tender age ruined her health and stunted her mind so that she was never afterward a normal person.

Spring came. The orchards burst into bloom, there were flowers in the meadow, and the fields were ready for sowing, but still the afflicted children writhed in torment and farming was forgotten in the frenzied search for new victims. The evidence against the witches became more elaborate and specific as the children became more accomplished. It was now known that the witches met regularly in a meadow belonging to Reverend Parris. It was a marshy place, infested with spade-foot frogs, which in spring and summer set up a diabolical clamor after nightfall. At midnight, an elfin horn was sounded from this place. Although God-fearing folk could not hear it, those who were in association with the Devil, even as far away as Andover and Salisbury, mounted their broomsticks at the first blast and came flying across the treetops to the pasture. Here they stuck their brooms, or besoms, in the soft earth of the marsh until it was time for the return journey.

The rites of the Sabbaths in the Parris orchard showed the Puritan influence. The European followers of Diana and Hecate would have scorned such sedate revels. The witches munched modestly on bread and cheese and then gathered in orderly meeting to listen to the Devil's word and partake of the Communion. None of the lurid obscenities of the European Black Mass were admitted in these meetings, which were not very different from those held in the meetinghouse on Sunday, except that the bread was red and the blood was real blood. The Devil even preached a sermon, a sort of evangelical harangue in which each witch was urged to go forth and make at least one convert before the next meeting. All this was reconstructed from the "confessions" of the witches and the second sight of the bewitched children.

It was in the Parris orchard that Ann Putnam first reported seeing "the little black minister" who officiated over these meetings as the grand wizard of all Massachusetts. Later Abigail Williams saw him, too, standing in the village street. She shouted that the black minister was there, and a farmer carrying a pitchfork hurled it at the spot to which she pointed. Abigail said that he had almost got the wizard, that she had heard his greatcoat tear. The children—with much difficulty, for black hands choked them whenever they tried to give this information—said that his name was George Burroughs. The Reverend George Burroughs was a retired minister living with his wife and seven children in Maine. But all his ministerial dignity and his study of theology counted as nothing in the face of these accusations.

When the Reverend George Burroughs mounted to the gallows on August 19, he delivered a last sermon which brought tears to the eyes of many; he ended by reciting the Lord's Prayer, gravely and faultlessly. This was something which it was believed no witch or wizard could do. One of the girls screamed that the Devil was prompting him, but since the Devil cannot say the Lord's Prayer either, this accusation carried little weight. The crowd might have been swayed to such pity that they would have stopped the execution, had not Cotton Mather, all in black on a black horse, risen in his stirrups and reminded them in a stirring voice that "the Devil is never more subtly himself than when he appears like an angel of light." The muttering of the crowd ceased and the sheriff proceeded with the hanging.

There must have been many solid citizens who realized that their neighbors were being led astray by hysterical adolescents. However, anyone who opposed the witch hunters or voiced doubts as to the validity of the tortures which the children were suffering would soon find himself accused of being a witch. Since the word of the children was taken as proof against any protestation of respectable adults, it was much too dangerous to speak out against the witch hunting. When magistrates, judges, and eminent divines of the neighborhood were seriously and unstintingly devoting their efforts to the cause, a simple farmer with only common sense to guide him dared not speak out.

One of the original "victims" of witchery, Mary Warren, came to repent of her folly and made a feeble attempt to make amends. She was maidservant to the John Proctors, and when her master—and, rumor had it, also her lover—was accused by some of the other girls, Mary was ready to tell the truth. She confessed that she had merely been bent upon sport and that she and the other girls "did but dissemble." Her confession was taken as a sign that the witches had tortured her into joining them. When Mary realized that her honesty was likely to land her in prison with the accused rather than in an honored seat in the courtroom, with ministers and judges doing her homage, she recanted. John Proctor was hanged and Mary rejoined the other girls in their yowling and writhing.

By now the fame of the girls had spread far beyond Salem village. Eminent divines—notably Cotton Mather, of Boston—came to investigate the case. Other towns called upon the girls to aid in identifying witches who were plaguing them. They journeyed to Andover, where they were received with awe and respect. Their courtroom technique was now becoming perfected. They went into a sort of trance in which they all did everything that the accused upon the witness stand did. If the defendant turned her head and raised her hand to her mouth, all the girls did so too, in a compulsive, agonized gesture, as though they could not help themselves. This was taken as sure proof that the witch was affecting them.

Another method of proof—and at the same time of breaking the witch's spell—called for the bewitched person to touch the witch who was tormenting her. The physical contact was supposed to free the victim, if it was indeed the accused who was causing the torments. On numerous occasions, one of the afflicted children would be carried, shrieking in agony, up to the witch and forced to touch her. There would be a final howl of anguish and then the victim would be quiet, indicating that the spell was broken and that the evil had passed back into the witch.

Abigail Williams and Ann Putnam were the two most talented witch finders. Abigail excelled in violence. She had the liveliest convulsions and had on several occasions terrified the Parris household by rushing to the fireplace and throwing firebrands around the room. Ann had the keenest discernment and could give vivid descriptions of what went on at the witches' meetings. Her testimony was particularly valued.

All through the summer and autumn of 1692 the witch trials continued. This farming community so neglected the fields during that hectic summer that winter supplies of grain became dangerously low. Perhaps this practical need helped to bring the community to its senses. By the spring of 1693, the fever had abated. Many of the witches who still languished in prison awaiting trials were allowed to go home. Tituba was among those released, being turned over to a new master who was willing to pay her jail fees in return for her lifetime services. The Puritan prisons charged the inmates board and room, and prisoners were not released if they could not meet the bill. A few of the witches, who had no friends or relatives to bail them out, died in prison. Financial restitution was made to the families of a number of those who had been executed.

Revulsion against the witch trials came gradually but steadily. There was bitter feeling against Reverend Parris for his part in the trials. The relatives of the jailed and executed refused to attend meeting so long as he was in the pulpit. Although he asked forgiveness for his crimes, he was eventually forced to leave the parish.

In 1696, Samuel Sewall, the Boston judge who had been one of the most active magistrates in prosecuting the witches, made his confession of error at the Old South Meeting in Boston. He stood before the congregation, his head bowed in shame, while the pastor read the confession Sewall had written of his part in the Salem witch trials.

Cotton Mather, however, never retracted his position. He continued to write pamphlets to justify his acts and attempted to promote further witch scares. But by this time the Puritan conscience had gained ascendancy over superstition and Mather merely made himself a laughingstock.

The real end of the Salem affair came on an August Sunday in 1706, the fourteenth anniversary of the fast and prayer which was held on behalf of the bewitched girls. Ann Putnam, now a woman of twenty-six, rose from her place in the meeting and stood with downcast eyes while the Reverend Joseph Green, Parris' successor, read her confession and public plea for forgiveness to those she had wronged. "It was a great delusion of Satan that deceived me in that sad time. . . . I did it not out of any anger, malice, or ill will." No one knows how the kinsfolk of Rebecca Nurse, who had been hanged because of the yowls of a twelve-year-old child, felt as they listened to this confession, but they were all there at the meeting. "I desire to lie in the dust and earnestly beg forgiveness of all those unto whom I have given just cause of sorrow and offense, whose relatives were taken away and accused," the confession went on. The congregation heard and granted its pardon.

Ann Putnam's confession did not mark the end of all witch hunting in New England, but never again was there a serious outbreak of this sort of hysteria in the New World. The fact that the prime movers in this affair recanted and apologized and that indemnities were paid to relatives of the victims not only had a very salutary effect in quenching further witch accusations in the colonies but also had wholesome repercussions in Europe.

The Philadelphia *Gazette* for October 15, 1730, reports a witch trial which took place at Mount Holly on October 12 of that year. Since the *Gazette* was at this time edited and almost entirely written by Benjamin Franklin, it is more than likely that he wrote this account himself. It is interesting to compare the humorous, tongue-in-cheek attitude of the Philadelphia report with that of the witch tract published in Northampton, England, in 1705, only twenty-five years earlier. It is clear that the colonies had come a long way since Cotton Mather's fanatical rantings on Gallows Hill and that the "crude" colonists were freer of superstition and bigotry than the people of Mother England.

Witchcraft in New England

The account in the *Gazette* reads as follows:

October 12, 1730. Saturday last at Mount Holly, near three hundred people were gathered together to see an experiment or two tried on some persons accused of witchcraft. It seems the accused had been charged with making their neighbors' sheep dance in an uncommon manner, and with causing hogs to speak and sing psalms, etc., to the great terror and amazement of the King's good and peaceful subjects in this province, and the accusers being very positive that if the accused were weighed in a scales against a Bible, the Bible would prove too heavy for them; or that, if they were bound and put into the water they would swim. The said accused, desirous to make their innocence appear, voluntarily offered to undergo the said trials, if two of the most violent of their accusers be tried with them. [Imagine such a suggestion being made at a trial conducted by Matthew Hopkins, Witch Finder General, or by Cotton Mather!]

Accordingly the time and place was agreed on, and advertised about the county. The accusers were one man and one woman, and the accused the same. The parties being met and the people got together, a grand consultation was held before they proceeded to trial; in which it was agreed to use the scales first, and a committee of men were appointed to search the men and a committee of women to search the women, to see if they had anything of weight about them, particularly pins. After the scrutiny was over, a huge great Bible, belonging to the Justice of the place, was provided and a lane thru the populace was made from the Justice's house to the scales, which were fixed on a gallows erected for that purpose opposite the house, that the Justice's wife and the rest of the ladies might see the trial without coming among the mob; and after the manner of Moorfield, a large ring was made.

Then came out of the house a grave tall man carrying the Holy Writ before the supposed Wizard (as solemnly as the Sword-bearer of London before the Lord Mayor). The wizard was first put in the scale and over him was read a chapter out of the Book of Moses, and then the Bible was put in the other scale (which being kept down before) was immediately let go. But to the great surprise of the spectators, flesh and blood came down plump and outweighed that great book by abundance. After the same manner the others were served, and their lumps of mortality were severally too heavy for Moses and all the Prophets and Apostles.

This being over, the accusers and the rest of the mob, not satisfied with this experiment, would have the trial by water. Accordingly a most solemn procession was made to the mill-pond, where both accused and accusers being stripp'd (saving only to the women their shifts) were bound hand and foot and severally placed in the water, lengthwise, from the side of a barge or flat, having for security only a rope about the middle of each, which was held by some in the flat. The accuser man, being thin and spare, with some difficulty began to sink at last; but the rest, every one of them, swam very light upon the water. A sailor in the flat jumped upon the back of the man accused, thinking to drive him to the bottom, but the person bound, without any help, came up some time before the other. The woman accuser, being told she did not sink . . . declared that she believed the accused had bewitched her to make her so light, and that she would be ducked again a hundred times, but that she would duck the devil out of her. The accused man, being surprised at his own swimming, was not so confident of his innocence as before, but said: "If I am a witch, it is more than I know."

The more thinking part of the spectators were of the opinion that any person so bound and placed in the water (unless they were mere skin and bones) would swim till their breath was gone and their lungs filled with water. But it being the general belief of the populace that the women's shifts, and the garters with which they were bound, helped to support them, it is said they are to be tried again the next warm weather, naked.

This bit of Franklinesque journalism shows that "the more thinking part" of the people were beginning to use common sense rather than hysterical judgment in these matters. In general Americans may feel more pride than shame in reviewing this country's share in the witch hysteria. Even the Salem outbreak was a small one compared to the holocausts in Europe during the seventeenth century. It is to be hoped that, if the people of the United States must be prey to hysteria in times of uncertainty and stress, as all peoples are, we can always regain our equilibrium as quickly as the Puritans did, that we will always have Franklins in the press gallery to quell hysteria with ridicule, and that, after the harm is done, we will have the grace to apologize and make what restitution we can for our injustices.

Come forth ye lass and trousered kid,
From prisoned mischief raise the lid,
And lift it good and high.

—JOHN KENDRICK BANGS, "Halloween"

12. The love tests of Halloween.

(Courtesy of the New York Public Library)

13. Snap apple night.

(Courtesy of the Bettmann Archive, New York)

"Trick or Treat"

THE CELEBRATION OF HALLOWEEN came rather late to the New World. Belief in witch-craft and the procedure for trying witches came over with the Pilgrims, but that reverend body rejected all church holidays—even Christmas. They certainly must have regarded Allhallows as popish nonsense, and the pranks and spells of the Gaelic Halloween would have been viewed with horror as work of the Devil.

The early settlers of America were predominantly English and Protestant, so that neither Allhallows nor Halloween were among their traditions. Halloween, as we have said, is a Gaelic, not an English, holiday. Although the Church of England recognizes All Saints' Day, the supernatural, roistering Halloween is not an English custom. In England, Guy Fawkes Day, celebrated November 5, takes the place of Halloween. This celebration is named after a historic event, but it follows much the same ancient autumn festival patterns as Halloween.

Guy Fawkes Day commemorates the discovery of the Gunpowder Plot, in 1605. Because of the anti-Catholic decrees of King James I, a plot was fomented to assassinate him by exploding a barrel of gunpowder in the House of Parliament when he was present. A number of men were involved in this plot, but Guy Fawkes was the one in charge of the actual explosion. He was apprehended in time and tortured into a confession.

On Guy Fawkes Day, the English dance in the streets carrying a scaffold from which hangs an effigy of the "Guy." Children masquerade and beg for "a penny for the Guy." In the evening there are bonfires and fireworks.

Halloween did not find a place on the American calendar of holidays until after the Gaelic people began to arrive on these shores. With them came the Catholic observance of Allhallows and All Souls and also the folklore about which still clung shreds of the ancient Vigil of Samhain and the Halloween sports of the fairy folk. These later colonists began the custom of holding gatherings at the farmhouses on the night of October 31. Since this was the time when apples and nuts were ripe, these two delicacies were an important feature of such parties. Halloween was often called "Snap Apple Night" or "Nutcrack Night" in pioneer days. The participants played the traditional divination games with nuts on the hearth, ducked for apples, threw apple peelings over their shoulders to determine the initials of their future bridegrooms, and indulged in other folk customs from the old country. They also discovered that the American pumpkins were excellent for making jack-o'-lanterns, and these carved pumpkin faces became traditional for Halloween.

These gatherings, however, were scattered and regional. It was not until after the great Irish immigration which followed the potato famine in the 1840's that Halloween really became a nationally observed holiday in the United States. Since the Irish believe that the "little people" are constantly hovering about the homes of mortals and that they are especially active on Halloween, any mischief that occurs on that night can be blamed on them. This is the background for the Halloween vandalism which reached its heights in the late 1800's. In lusty pioneer communities, practical jokes were one of the favorite diversions at any time of year, and Halloween provided splendid opportunity for this form of amusement. Honest householders on the morning of November 1 were very likely to find their wagon on the barn roof, the front gate hanging in a sycamore tree, and the outhouse lying on its side. "The goblins must have done it."

This vandalism has abated considerably in this generation. It has been suggested that the prevalence of indoor plumbing has taken much of the sport out of Halloween. Also, the police, in spite of being predominantly Irish in ancestry in this country, take a dim view of goblins and lay a heavy hand on the real culprit when they can catch him. However, any prudent person will see to it that his car is locked in the garage and his porch furniture stowed away before Halloween night.

The predominant Halloween practice at present is for gangs of children in each neighborhood to dress up in outlandish costumes with weird masks and to go from house to house ringing doorbells and shouting, "Anything for the goblins?" or "Trick or treat?"

There are numerous precedents for this Halloween masking and begging. It may stem from the "souling" and "penny for the Guy" activities in England. Wood-Martin, in *Traces of the Elder Faiths of Ireland*, recounts a form of "trick or treat" which was carried on in Ireland until after the turn of this century. On the eve of Samhain, the rustics in the district between Ballycotton and Trabolgan paraded through the district, stopping at each farmhouse to levy contributions in the name of "Muck Olla." The identity of Muck Olla has been lost in the mists of the past, but the name is probably a perversion of that of some old Druid god; certainly it comes from pagan times. The procession was led by a man in a white robe wearing a horse-head mask. (The horse was sacred to the Sun God, which indicates that this custom was a survival of a Druid rite.) This master of ceremonies was called Lair Bhan (White Mare). After him walked young men blowing cows' horns, with the remainder of the procession trailing behind this group.

At each house the procession halted, called out the master, and recited a long string of verses, the purport of which was that the farmer's prosperity was due to the goodness of Muck Olla and that if he wished to continue to prosper he had best make a generous contribution to that spirit. They went on with a dire description of what would happen if Muck Olla's messengers were not treated with respect and liberality. The farmers took no chances with Muck Olla's vengeance and made liberal contributions, mostly in kind. The procession staggered happily home at the end of the evening, laden with butter, eggs, corn, potatoes, and other farm produce.

It has also been suggested that the Halloween masquerading may stem from a medieval custom of celebrating Allhallows. On this day, dedicated to the memory of the saints, each church displayed in a solemn procession the relics of the saint who was its patron. However, as the churches grew more numerous, there were not enough genuine relics to go around; especially as some wealthy parishes, such as that of the castle church at Wittenberg, collected sacred relics by the thousands. Newer and poorer parishes, therefore, having no relics to display, masqueraded in representation of their patron saints. Those who were not playing the parts of the holy ones also wanted to get into the procession, and so they dressed up as angels or devils. The Allhallows procession around the churchyard eventually became a gay and motley parade.

Whatever the custom stems from, the wise householder will see to it that he has a stock of apples, candies, or pennies on hand for Halloween night, for if he slams the door on the group of oddly dressed midgets who ring his bell that night it is very likely that the next morning he will find soap scrawls on his windows, flour on his front steps, and the shrubbery wreathed in toilet paper.

Halloween has now become what the sociologists refer to as a degenerate holiday. Although there are those faithful who attend mass that day, it is a time devoted chiefly to the delight and amusement of children. Witches and their black arts are no longer a menace in the community. Ghosts, well aware that no offerings are laid out for them by their relatives, haunt their former homes no more on October 31. Fairies exist only between the covers of brightly illustrated books for children.

Despite all this, shreds of the old pagan superstitions still cling to us all. We can still feel a glow of satisfaction when, at a Halloween gathering, the nut we have named for our best beloved burns quietly on the hearth next to our own; and our heart beats a little faster when the apple peeling thrown over the shoulder traces the initial of our true love. And, although of course you do not believe in ghosts, would you dare to walk alone through a graveyard on Halloween night?

I N D E X

Index

Index